The Impact of Coincidence in Modern American, British, and Asian History

Anthem Impact provides a vehicle for authors wishing to publish original, peer-reviewed scholarly and scientific research at a significantly shorter length than previous publishing models have allowed (20,000-30,000 words). Expertly written by recognized authorities and regularly updated, these reference titles offer researchers, graduate students and practitioners in-depth, high-level research and the latest thinking on a range of specialized topics across a variety of subject areas. Available in both digital and print formats, titles include critical, succinct surveys of the current state of research, advanced introductions on emerging subjects and/or original, cutting edge insights into frontier topics.

The Impact of Coincidence in Modern American, British, and Asian History: Twenty-One Unusual Historical Events

Bruce A. Elleman

ANTHEM PRESS

Anthem Press
An imprint of Wimbledon Publishing Company
www.anthempress.com

This edition first published in UK and USA 2023
by ANTHEM PRESS
75–76 Blackfriars Road, London SE1 8HA, UK
or PO Box 9779, London SW19 7ZG, UK
and
244 Madison Ave #116, New York, NY 10016, USA

© 2023 Bruce Elleman

British Library Cataloguing-in-Publication Data
A catalogue record for this book is available from the British Library.

Library of Congress Control Number: 2023940004
A catalog record for this book has been requested.

ISBN-13: 978-1-83998-960-5 (Pbk)
ISBN-10: 1-83998-960-2 (Pbk)

Cover Credit: Battle of Gallipoli image from Wikimedia commons

This title is also available as an e-book.

To Jason Ehrenberg. For keeping me employed at the U.S. Naval War College long enough to finish this book.

CONTENTS

INTRODUCTION: THE UNINTENTIONAL ROLE OF COINCIDENCE IN HISTORY

Research conducted in National Archives, University Libraries and Presidential Libraries often unearth documents of great interest, but of uncertain historical validity. Are these random documents important, or incidental to the events of their time? It can be hard to tell. Sometimes it is impossible to know for sure. Often, they appear to explain unexplained events. They can even appear to add the dot to the "i" or the cross to the "t." But without corroborating documents they might be "false flags." Or perhaps even complete forgeries, with the sole goal of deceiving and throwing researchers off the trail. How can one tell the difference?

Collected in this short book are 21 examples of "coincidental" history. Many were originally classified, or simply buried deep in archives. These historical tidbits were gathered during almost 40 years of research, in such unlikely places as the Lenin Library in Moscow, the Peking University Library in Beijing, Academia Sinica in Taiwan, the Foreign Ministry Archives in Tokyo, the UK National Archives at Kew and the British Library in London. Within the United States, I conducted research at the Herbert Hoover, FDR, Truman, Eisenhower, JFK, Johnson, Nixon, Ford, Carter, Reagan, and Bush Presidential Libraries and Archives, in approximately that order. I have also used both the National Archives in College Park, Maryland, plus at the downtown Manuscript Collection of the Library of Congress. Many personal papers were left to institutional archives, like the Hoover Archives at Stanford, the Rare Book Library at Columbia and the Houghton Library at Harvard.

After a 40-year career, I have visited dozens of archives, libraries and private collections. To date, 34 books have already been published including the fruits of my labors, with another 8 volumes (including this one) on my to-do list. Many of the stories in this book do not fit seamlessly into regular histories, because they are not provable. Rather than allow these historical tidbits to be lost, however, I have decided to publish them as a set. Twenty-one seemed an appropriate number, since in many world cultures the combination of three "7s" are deemed lucky; for example, Japan attacked China on 7 July 1937, or 7-7-7. But a word of warning before an eager reader begins: none of these 21 coincidental documentary tales tell the full story. At the best they might help illuminate unexplained historical mysteries. But at the worst they might possibly deceive. Therefore let the reader beware: take each of these chapters with an appropriate "grain of salt"!

Chapter 1

SECRET U.S. PLANS TO ABSORB HAWAII AND GUAM (1897)

The Pacific Ocean has three major North-South island chains, including the so-called "first island chain" that runs from the tip of the Kamchatka Peninsula down through the Kurile Islands, the Japanese home islands, Okinawa, Taiwan and on through to the Philippines. The so-called "second island chain" splits away from Japan, and runs southward toward the Bonins, Guam and the Marshall Islands. Meanwhile, the so-called "third island chain" runs from the end of the Aleutian Trench southward along the Emperor Seamount, through Midway, and ends up in the Hawaiian Islands (see Map 1).

During the late nineteenth century, Japan expanded along the first and second island chains and into the Western Pacific. In 1876, Japan obtained all of the Kurile Islands in exchange for ceding the southern half of Sakhalin Island to Russia, and also seized the Bonin Islands, about 1,300 kilometers to the southeast of Japan. In 1879, the Ryukyu Islands were formally annexed by Japan and became the prefecture of Okinawa. Finally, after the first Sino-Japanese War (1894–95), Japan obtained the island of Taiwan—in theory in perpetuity—in 1895, which gave it unbroken control from Kamchatka to Taiwan. Japan's expansion effectively cut the U.S. sea line of communication (SLOC) to China, which was considered to be a major trading partner.

In 1897, assistant secretary of the Navy, Theodore Roosevelt, and Commander C. J. Goodrich, president, U.S. Naval War College (NWC), carried on a confidential correspondence discussing how Japan's recent expansion impacted the United States. The original letters are in the NWC Historical Archives. On 23 June 1897, Goodrich explained that a Japanese attack on the United States would have to be staged from either Dutch Harbor (Unalaska) in the Aleutians or from Hawaii:

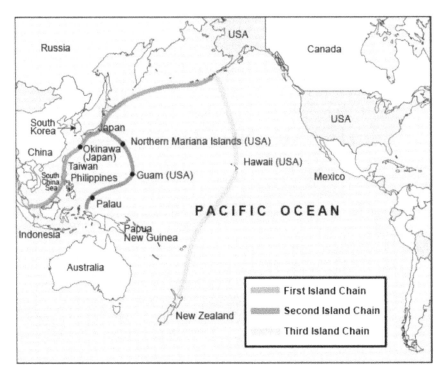

Map 1 The three island chains.

Honolulu, on the other hand, is the bone of contention, and therefore
a principal objective point. Though farther than Unalaska from Japan,
it can be approached by stages, Midway, or one of the adjacent islands
being occupied for a base of coaling station whence to operate against
Honolulu, only 1,000 miles or so distant. Such a course of action by
Japan would force the United States to operate at a distance of 2,000
miles from its own coast.

Even after U.S. forces took Hawaii in a U.S.-Japanese War, Japan could still
"profit by the exceptional facilities for approach afforded her by the scattered
islands lying to the westward of the Hawaiian group."[1]

Coincidentally, during the very next year, in the midst of the 1898 Spanish-
American War, which was nominally being fought over Cuba, Washington
used the war with Spain as its rationale to annex Hawaii outright and invade

---

1 Captain C. F. Goodrich, "Letter to Assistant Secretary on War with Japan," 23 June
   1897, XSTP, U.S. Naval War College Historical Archives, 7 pages, plus two appendices.

Guam and the Philippines. By the 10 December 1898 Treaty of Paris, Spain ceded the Philippine Islands to the United States for $20 million, while Guam became a permanent U.S. territory. In a single stroke, the United States consolidated control over strategic bases on the third, second and first island chains and in so doing reopened a direct naval route to China. Arguably, this was the real reason for fighting the war with Spain; Cuba was just a convenient diversion.

During World War II, the United States and Japan continued to fight for control over the three island chains, beginning with Honolulu, Hawaii. Only after their victory at Midway, however, could U.S. forces begin to move from the third island chain into Japan's outermost security sphere, referred to as the "Region of Defence," based on control of the second island chain; next, attack its lines of communication bringing essential goods from the "Region of Supplies," which depended on unbroken control over the first island chain, and finally attack the so-called "Inner Ring" that encompassed the Japanese home islands, Okinawa, Taiwan, Manchukuo and eastern China (see Map 2).

After the war, the United States granted the Philippines independence in 1946, but retained its strategic bases on Hawaii, Guam and especially Okinawa, which still hosts 75% of U.S. bases in Japan in terms of area, even though Okinawa represents just 0.6% of Japan's total territory.

Chinese policymakers are actively studying the nineteenth- and twentieth-century history of the three island chains and surely realize that it is by retaining strategic dominance over the first, second and third island chains that the United States has been allowed to enjoy unparalleled sea control over the Pacific Ocean. Even though America remains the principal sea power in the Pacific, the PRC's recent naval investments appear aimed at undermining this authoritative position, beginning with the first island chain.

The key to China's maritime strategy is Taiwan. Jiang Zhijun, director of the Chinese Naval Research Institute of the PLA Navy, stated in 2002:

> Taiwan is China's ideal seaward exit way bequeathed to us by our ancestors. As long as Taiwan is in China's hand, then the Pacific would be an open area to China. Taiwan itself is a key link in the "first island chain." After Taiwan is reunified with mainland China, this "first island chain" blockade will be broken, enabling the Chinese troops to expand their defense lines out to the Pacific in the East in order to better protect the safety of China's coast and inland.

However, according to Jiang, taking Taiwan is not the end, but just the beginning:

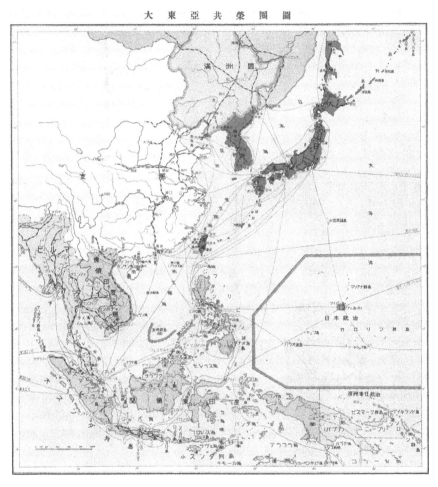

大　東　亞　共　榮　圏　圖

Map 2 Japan's sphere of co-prosperity, 1938.

Once the (Taiwan) reunification mission is completed, Diaoyu (Senkaku) Island to the North and the waters surrounding it would fall into the range of the Chinese gunfire protection. To the south, the distance from China's coastal defense force to all the South China Sea islands and regions will be shortened by a big margin.[2]

This Chinese expansionist policy in many respects simply reverse mirror images what the United States accomplished in the 1898 Spanish-American War. In other words, it is highly reminiscent of Goodrich's secret 23 June 1897 letter to Teddy Roosevelt.

---

2 *People's Liberation Daily*, 2 January 2004.

Chapter 2

ALFRED THAYER MAHAN INVENTS ISLAND-HOPPING (1911)

The NWC Historical Archives also show that, in 1911, Alfred Thayer Mahan wrote to R. P. Rodgers, president, U.S. Naval War College, to explain that if Japan occupied and fortified a large number of Pacific islands, then it would be "tied to supporting them" and "It might even be urged as a sound policy on the part of Blue [U.S.], to induce Orange [Japan] to such distant effort, which would place it in the same position the Blue finds so difficult in trans-Pacific operations."[1] Mahan's idea had much in common with the Asian game of "Wei-ch'i" in China, or "Go" in Japan, which unlike Western games like Chess sought to take strategic territory so as to surround the enemy's bases, not to destroy them directly by a frontal assault but to render them ineffective. Coincidentally, during World War II many Japanese bases on various Pacific Islands were not attacked, but were hopped over, surrounded and over time "withered on the vine."

Mahan also proposed the concept of "island hopping." On 4 March 1911, Mahan told Rodgers: "In short, I believe Blue can recover a base, and gradually recover all captured positions [from Orange] in such order as may seem expedient. Some [Japanese island bases] may be even neglected, as immaterial, in favor of offensive action against the enemy's positions"[2] (see Picture 1).

In a 22 February 1911 letter, Mahan made this strategy of skipping over certain Japanese bases even more clear when he discussed holding a certain island base as "a stepping stone to a base in or near the Orange territory, from which the superior Blue fleet can operate offensively as may be judged most expedient." Mahan's top choice for this Blue base was the island of Okinawa: "An anchorage in the LuChus [Okinawa] is the most effective position for the

---

1 These three letters from Alfred Thayer Mahan were addressed to Rear Admiral R. P. Rodgers, president of the Naval War College, and dated 22 February, 4 March and 17 March 1911, U.S. Naval War College Historical Archives.
2 Ibid.

Picture 1 Portrait of Alfred Thayer Mahan.

Blue Fleet." Further, if Guam was skipped on the way to Okinawa, this would not matter much, since by taking Okinawa all communications to the south would be crippled and so this "would probably cause the recall of [Japanese] cruisers based on Guam [...]."[3]

If the Japanese occupied Hawaii, Mahan suggested that the "Blue battle fleet remains there" to hold the Japanese forces in place, which would provide a buffer for "the armored cruisers proceeding against Guam."[4] This too revealed a strategy based on bypassing a crucial Japanese position in order to cut its lines of communication, thus undermining its logistical supply line and making its position more and more untenable. When taking back these islands, the U.S. Navy could then jump over those it did not need, leaving them to "wither on the vine."

Coincidentally, in the early days of World War II, Japan used its Pacific island bases to push the United States off of Guam, invaded the Philippines, plus attacked Hawaii. The strategy adopted by the U.S. Navy to defeat Japanese forces in the Pacific relied on Mahan's island-hopping proposal from

---

3 Ibid.
4 Ibid.

1911. His suggestion that the United States should "deceive" the Japanese into fortifying as many Pacific island bases as possible also would appear to have been adopted. For example, after WWI, the United States did not resist when Japan built bases on its mandate islands in the Carolines, Marianas, Marshall and Palau.

Mahan's core idea in 1911 was then to bypass strongly fortified bases held by the Japanese, thereby incurring fewer battle losses and also effectively cutting off Japanese-occupied areas. According to Edward Miller, "Rabaul and Truk, Japan's two great outlying bases, were outflanked and left in the wake of the fleet. The bypassing of citadels on such a grand scale was almost unprecedented in the history of warfare."[5] Important victories using this strategy arguably included Guadalcanal (1942); Tarawa (1943); Kwajalein, Saipan, Guam, and Leyte Gulf (1944); and Iwo Jima and Okinawa (1945).

Based on these secret 1911 letters, it appears certain that Mahan himself was the first to suggest utilizing the "island hopping" strategy. More to the point, he did so as part of a larger plan of deception aimed at convincing Japan that it should build up its Pacific island bases, and thereby induce "Orange to such distant effort, which would place it in the same position the Blue finds so difficult in trans-Pacific operations." By simultaneously urging Japan to pour its limited resources into fortifying island bases, even while formulating a strategy that made such bases unimportant or even a liability, Mahan appears to have single-handedly created what would prove to be a winning strategy for World War II.

---

5 Edward S. Miller, *War Plan Orange: The U.S. Strategy to Defeat Japan 1897–1945* (Annapolis, MD: Naval Institute Press, 2007), 351.

Chapter 3

YUAN SHIKAI PREAPPROVES JAPAN'S "21 DEMANDS" (1915)

Yuan Shikai (Yuan Shih-kai) was one to the most significant Chinese political figures in the late nineteenth and early twentieth centuries (see Picture 2). He was a high military official of the Qing Dynasty who turned against it, succeeded Sun Yatsen as the first president of the Chinese Republic and then attempted to found a new imperial dynasty by signing the so-called "21 Demands" with Japan. Coincidentally, his rival Sun Yatsen claimed Yuan Shikai proposed these demands to Japan, not the other way around. When his attempt to become emperor failed, Yuan Shikai died soon afterwards under mysterious circumstances.

Although retired from the Qing Army, when the Double Ten (October 10th) Revolution began in 1911, the Qing dynasty summoned General Yuan Shikai back to duty. Yuan was appointed to command an army to suppress the rebellion. However, Yuan was in no rush and declined to accept the appointment, saying a foot injury still troubled him. Yuan was finally persuaded to take up the command of the army in return for the office of prime minister. Yuan then entered into negotiations with the rebels and he played the Qing court off the politically naive revolutionary leader Sun Yatsen. By March 1912, the Manchus had abdicated and Yuan was named first president of the Republic of China (ROC).

Over the next two years, Yuan Shikai engaged in political intrigue subverting the democratic government. After destroying the revolutionaries' political and military authority, Yuan moved to consolidate his power. He dissolved the National Assembly, replacing it with a political council composed of his own cronies. This body created a constitutional council to draft a new governing document. But this new "constitution" in fact granted unlimited powers to the president.

The outbreak of World War I presented Yuan with new difficulties. As Western interest shifted away from East Asia, the Japanese were given a relatively free hand. As an ally of Great Britain, Japan seized the German territorial concessions in Qingdao, Shandong. During January 1915, the Japanese

Picture 2 Portrait of Yuan Shikai.

presented Yuan's government with their infamous 21 Demands, including full Japanese control over China's finances, police and many other government affairs. If all 21 demands had all been granted as written, China would have been transformed into little more than a Japanese protectorate. No foreign power intervened to stop Japan, however, and Yuan was unwilling to commit his army to fight the Japanese. Therefore, he submitted to all but the most radical of these demands.

Coincidentally, Yuan's opponent Sun Yatsen was also negotiating with Japan at the time. Arguably, this gave Japan added leverage. When the 21 Demands were announced, Sun insisted that they had not been drafted by the Japanese at all, but by Yuan Shikai in return for Japanese favors. By agreeing to the 21 Demands, Yuan would obtain Japan's support for recognizing him as the new emperor of China. In a 1917 publication, Sun even accused Yuan: "In fact, the Twenty-one Demands were presented by Japan at his own instigation: Japan did not, in the beginning, press him to accept these demands."[1]

---

1 Sun Yatsen, *The Vital Problems of China* (Taipei: China Cultural Service, 1953 reprint), 55.

Coincidentally, evidence confirming Sun's accusation appeared in an unlikely place. As per the Woodrow Wilson papers, on 12 November 1917, W. G. Sharp, U.S. ambassador to China, reported to President Wilson that the idea that Japanese government had issued an "ultimatum" was merely a ploy to appease the Japanese people. In fact, a "considerable number of the original provisions of the ultimatum had been refused by China and others compatible to her dignity and security had been accepted." Only the ones acceptable to China were then called an "ultimatum." This charade then allowed Yuan Shikai to "keep face" by blaming Japan for the ultimatum even while obtaining Japan's support to become the new emperor[2] (see Document 1).

Yuan's desire to found a new imperial dynasty moved forward with Japan's support. The monarchical movement began in earnest in August 1915. By December 1915, Yuan was petitioned to ascend the throne and found a new dynasty. Orders were then issued transforming China from a republic to a monarchy. Unfortunately for Yuan, this move was met with domestic revolts and by March 1916 the monarchical experiment was over, and Yuan reluctantly restored a republican government. Throughout the spring, Yuan tried to negotiate a settlement with the military commanders in the southwest. In June 1916, exhausted and ill, Yuan died suddenly of uremia, a kidney disease. But even though Yuan failed to become China's new emperor, Japan kept its diplomatic gains. The Chinese government would later try its best to cancel the 21 Demands at the 1919 Paris Peace Conference.

2 Bruce A. Elleman, *Wilson and China: A Revised History of the Shandong Question* (Armonk, NY: M.E. Sharpe, 2002), 19.

PARIS, November 12, 1917

My dear Mr. President:

In my letter of some little time ago, after having dwelt upon conditions then prevailing in France, I promised to write you giving my observations concerning some of the problems confronting the allies having to do with their relations toward each other.

Mr. Hoo Wei Teh said that he strongly believed it was Japanese intrigue that later fomented the disturbances in Southern China, with the object of furnishing an excuse for Japan to come in and establish order. He narrated in an amusing manner an interesting story of how, to appease the people of Japan, that Government had given out for home consumption the fact that an ultimatum had been given to China imposing certain conditions upon her which she would be compelled to accept. As a matter of fact, a considerable number of the original provisions of the ultimatum had been refused by China and others compatible to her dignity and security had been accepted. Those that had been accepted were proudly announced in Tokio as being the ultimatum to which Japan was soon going to force China to agree. A further phase of this international game lay in the fact that, while it had been solemnly enjoined upon the Chinese Government not to make known any of the rejected Articles of the so-called ultimatum which had been proposed, yet the British and other Governments at Pekin had been let into the "secret", that only the accepted provisions had been proposed to China.

As I am despatching this letter, I am reminded by its date that it should reach you on the eve of the day when the fine sentiments expressed in your Thanksgiving Day proclamation will be read from a number of the public places in Paris.

Believe me, dear Mr. President,

Very sincerely yours,

W. G. Sharp.

Document 1 W. G. Sharp telegram to Wilson.

Chapter 4

GALLIPOLI'S UNEXPECTED CONNECTION TO THE ARMENIAN GENOCIDE (1915)

The British World War I campaign against the Dardanelles was initially meant to be purely a naval effort, but its failure to force a passage through Turkey's defenses required a change of strategy. The new plan was to adopt a peripheral campaign to secure the Gallipoli Peninsula. If the originally planned 24 April 1915 landing was successful, land troops could clear away the Turkish shore emplacements and field artillery, and thus permit the passage of the British fleet to Constantinople. Coincidentally, on 24 April 1915 Turkey began to purge its Armenian minority in anticipation that as fellow Christians the Armenians might back the British against the Turks. Eventually, as many as a million Armenians died as a result of this Turkish repression.

General Sir Ian Hamilton, who was commander of Eastern Command, was in charge of the Gallipoli operation. He had serious doubts that a landing operation could succeed, and was warned that the Turks might fortify the coast, turning the operation into a "second Crimea," just like a similar landing disaster some 60 years earlier in the Crimean war.[1] Nevertheless, when Kitchener ordered the landing to be attempted, Hamilton decided that the Anzac force would land to the north of Gaba Tepe and the 29th Division would land at five beaches near Cape Helles. While the 29th went north, the Anzacs would advance east across the peninsula to block Turkish reinforcements.

---

1 Robin Prior, "Gallipoli as a combined and joint operation," in Bruce A. Elleman and S.C.M. Paine, Eds., *Naval Power and Expeditionary Warfare: Peripheral Campaigns and New Theatres of Naval Warfare* (New York: Routledge, 2012), 47; citing Hunter-Weston to Hamilton 30.3.15, Hamilton Papers, King's College, London, 17.7.30. Much of the description of the Gallipoli landing presented here is based on this chapter.

This plan was too complicated. By simultaneously landing at six different beaches, Hamilton hoped to confuse the Turkish defenses. But instead the landing parties quickly got bogged down. Rather than move immediately inland, the two forces landing at Helles Y and S beaches awaited the arrival of the main force from the south. Meanwhile, further to the north, the Anzac landing was just north of Gaba Tepe. Hamilton's mistake of not leaving the beaches immediately to attack the Turkish troops was to have dire consequences.

Among his many problems, Hamilton completely underestimated the Turkish response. In mid-March 1915, they formed a new Fifth Army commanded by General Liman von Sanders, former head of the German military mission to Turkey. Soon, the Turks had moved about 40,000 men and 100 artillery pieces to the west side of the peninsula ready to oppose the landing. The Turkish garrisons defending the peninsula were well dug in and most of the coastline from Morto Bay to Gaba Tepe was covered by a thin screen of troops.

On 25 April 1915, a day later than originally planned, British and Anzac forces landed on the Gallipoli Peninsula. The Turks could not dislodge them. But the landing parties could not break out either. They were trapped on the beaches. At beach Y, the Turkish command was so alarmed at the size of the landing—some 2,500 men—that their counterattacks forced a British troop withdrawal on the 26th. The other landings were more successful, however, but the forces soon became locked in place and the objective of crossing the peninsula *en masse* to threaten Constantinople was never achieved.

Coincidentally, the original landing date at Gallipoli was set for 24 April 1915. On that very date, the Turkish government began to round up and kill as many as one million Armenians, hoping to forestall any domestic support for the British (see Picture 3). Previous expeditionary landings similar to the one at Gallipoli showed the value of having local supporters. For example, in the Iberian campaign during the Napoleonic Wars the local population in Portugal and Spain supported Britain during the Napoleonic Wars or, more accurately, Britain supported the local population's fight against French domination. Together Wellington's conventional army and Spanish guerrilla forces put the French forces in the untenable position of having to concentrate to fight the conventional army while having to disperse to fight the insurgency. The Iberian geography impeded the arrival of French reinforcements, while its long coastline facilitating British operations by allowing efficient replenishment, deployment, and escape by sea. None of this would have been possible without a supportive local population.

Had the local Turkish population been equally friendly, Gallipoli might well have succeeded. Indeed, this possibility clearly occurred to the Ottomans,

Picture 3 Rounding up the Armenians.

since they massacred Armenians whom they perceived to be sympathetic to the Entente powers. The Ottomans did not want an internal hostile population assisting the British. The tragic Armenian genocide may have been an unintended consequence of Gallipoli. The Gallipoli operation was a strategic disaster. It is unclear if the British might have had more success if an Armenian rebellion had occurred simultaneously with the Gallipoli landing, but this never became a serious possibility following the Turkish crackdown on their Armenian minority.

Chapter 5

THE HISTORICAL IMPORTANCE OF 7 DECEMBER 1902/1917/1941

Sometimes dates can be used for sending signals. For example, on 7 December 1902 Germany and Great Britain instituted their "peaceful blockade" of Venezuela. On 7 December 1917, the U.S. Navy merged with the British Navy to fight Germany. On 7 December 1941, the Japanese simultaneously attacked the United States at Pearl Harbor and the British in Hong Kong and Singapore. Does this date hold a special significance for Great Britain, the United States and Japan? Or was it just a simple coincidence three times?

The Venezuelan Crisis of 1902–1903 threatened to pit the United States and Great Britain against each other. Venezuela's European creditors were firm in their demands that President Castro pay off Venezuela's mounting foreign debts. Several European nations sent their fleets, and on 25 November 1902 Germany and Great Britain formally announced their intention to implement a "pacific" blockade of Venezuela. It was widely assumed that such an action might result in foreign domination of Venezuela.

President Theodore Roosevelt opposed this action as a violation of the Monroe Doctrine, and the U.S. Navy's "winter exercise" of 1902–1903 was timed to correspond exactly with this German-British threat. The blockade was declared on 7 December 1902, and for "eleven days, between 8 December and 18 December 1902, the future of U.S., British, German, and Venezuelan relations hung in the balance as Theodore Roosevelt discreetly pursued diplomatic negotiations between Venezuela and the two great European powers."[1]

The U.S. Navy was able to mobilize 53 ships to counter the 29 ships available to Britain and Germany in the Caribbean. War appeared more and more likely. On 16 December 1902, Parliament convened to debate the

---

1 Henry J. Hendrix, "Overwhelming Force and the Venezuelan Crisis of 1902–1903," in Bruce A. Elleman and S.C.M. Paine, Eds., *Navies and Soft Power: Historical Case Studies of Naval Power and the Nonuse of Military Force* (Newport, RI: NWC Press, 2015), 21. Much of the description of the Venezuelan Crisis presented here is based on this chapter.

situation in Venezuela and the strains it was placing on Britain's relationship with America. Outnumbered and outgunned, on 17 December 1902, the two European nations conceded defeat, lifted the blockade and agreed to arbitrate the matter with Venezuela instead.

Great Britain's decision to back down had another, albeit unintended, result. The British Colonial Office drafted a secret memorandum raising questions about the defensibility of British possessions in the western Atlantic in the event of a conflict with the United States. The Admiralty response acknowledged that the United States would be in a position to "stop our supplies from Canada" and to secure all food imports from the United States itself, effectively cutting off two-thirds of Great Britain's food supply. The inescapable conclusion was "the necessity of preserving good relations with the United States."[2] Within two years Lansdowne and Balfour would secure an unofficial security arrangement with the United States, the beginning of what has come to be known as "the Special Relationship."[3]

Fifteen years later to the day, the U.S. Navy and the Royal Navy merged their ships on 7 December 1917 to fight Germany. Japan was also a British ally, but it was not asked to join; the Japanese probably felt excluded. After joining the war, the Americans quickly sent so-called "submarine chasers," which were employed in the English Channel and Strait of Otranto. In addition, they sent several obsolete American warships or converted yachts engaged in anti-submarine patrols or convoy duties working in the Bay of Biscay or from Gibraltar. But one of the most important U.S. Navy contributions to Great Britain took place at Queenstown. To ease logistical problems, coal-burning rather than oil-burning ships were sent to Queenstown, since Great Britain had ample supplies of domestic coal. In July 1917, after first obtaining the endorsement of Admiral William Sims, Admiral John Jellicoe, the First Sea Lord, requested a detachment of four American coal-burning dreadnoughts.[4] These American battleships would strengthen the Grand Fleet in its blockade of the German High Seas Fleet in the North Sea. They also would permit the British to retire some of their pre-dreadnoughts, thereby freeing up crews to man 119 new anti-submarine destroyers under construction in British yards.[5]

---

2 Ibid., citing "Caribbean Sea and Western Atlantic: Strategic Conditions in Event of War with the United States," BNA, Admiralty Group (ADM) 1/8875, 21 January 1903.

3 Ibid., citing William N. Tilchin, *Theodore Roosevelt and the British Empire: A Study in Presidential Statecraft* (New York: St. Martin's Press, 1997), 102–105.

4 Rear Admiral William Sowden Sims, *The Victory at Sea* (New York: Doubleday, 1920; reprinted Annapolis: Naval Institute Press, 1984), 349–350.

5 Jerry W. Jones, *U.S. Battleship Operations in World War I* (Annapolis: Naval Institute Press, 1998), 12.

The American destroyers arrived in Britain during November 1917. Sims and Jellicoe agreed that four American battleships would be attached to the Grand Fleet. For the first time, American warships were to be "integrated as subordinate units into a fleet commanded by an officer of the Royal Navy." After an extremely rough passage, *New York*, *Florida*, *Delaware*, and *Wyoming* steamed into the massive base of the British Grand Fleet in the roadstead of Scapa Flow in the Orkney Islands. Coincidentally, these two fleets merged on 7 December 1917, 15 years to the day after the Venezuelan blockade that resulted in the "special relationship" between the United States and Great Britain. Scholars later emphasized how that day's "marriage of American and British capital fleets lasted to the end of World War I in November 1918."[6]

Japan, of course, was also a close British naval ally in World War I. No similar invitation from the British government to Tokyo to merge Japanese ships with the British Grand Fleet was forthcoming. We know from the proceedings at the 1919 Paris Peace Conference that Japan felt the Western European nations and the United States often slighted Japan's participation, and did not treat the Japanese government with full racial equality. It is not too difficult to conclude, therefore, that the racially sensitive Japanese Navy might have felt excluded. Thus, 24 years later to the day, also coincidentally on 7 December 1941, Japan simultaneously attacked the U.S. naval base at Pearl Harbor and British naval bases in Hong Kong and Singapore. Was this third appearance of 7 December also a simple coincidence? Or did the 7 December date have a deeper historical meaning for Japan? Was Tokyo, perhaps, sending the United States and United Kingdom a "special" message of its own, reminding them how it had been purposefully excluded on 7 December 1917?

---

6 Kenneth J. Hagan and Michael T. McMaster, "The Anglo-American Naval Checkmate of Germany's *Guerre de Course*, 1917–1918," in Bruce A. Elleman and S.C.M. Paine, Eds., *Commerce Raiding: Historical Case Studies, 1755–2009* (Newport, RI: NWC Press, 2013), 159. Much of the description of the two navies merging presented here is based on this chapter.

Chapter 6

THE HALIFAX EXPLOSION
AND UNIFICATION OF THE U.S.
AND BRITISH NAVIES (1917)

Obtaining the United States as an ally was the major prize for the British in December 1917, since it brought significant potential naval resources that might win the war against Germany. American ships, notably older coal-burning destroyers sent to Queenstown soon after the American entry into the war, made a huge difference; by the end of August, there were 35 ships total. The formal unification of the British and American fleets on 7 December 1917 was coincidentally proceeded by a chance munitions explosion in Halifax, Canada, on 6 December 1917 (see Picture 4). Once Britain's main naval base in North America was destroyed, and there was no possibility of ever using America's ships against her, the unification of the two navies proceeded as planned the very next day.

The 6 December 1917 munitions explosion that destroyed Halifax was caused by an American-leased ship. One of the first large-scale humanitarian aid missions by sea occurred during World War I with the creation of the non-profit Commission for the Relief of Belgium (CRB). This aid organization distributed $927,681,485.08 worth of foodstuffs and clothing to Belgium and to German-occupied areas of Northern France. Because of the Commission's almost total reliance on international shipping, the CRB was once described by critics as a "piratical state organized for benevolence": "Like a pirate state, the CRB flew its own flag, negotiated its own treaties, secured special passports, fixed prices, issued currency, and exercised a great deal of fiscal independence."[1]

---

1 Bruce A. Elleman, "Starvation Blockade and Herbert Hoover's commission for relief in Belgium, 1914–1919," in Bruce A. Elleman and S.C.M. Paine, Eds., *Navies and Soft Power: Historical Case Studies of Naval Power and the Nonuse of Military Force* (Newport, RI: NWC Press, 2015), 47--67. Much of the description of the CRB activities presented here are based on this chapter.

Picture 4 Aftermath of the Halifax explosion.

The director, future U.S. president Herbert Hoover, had to obtain permission first from England and Germany to let the aid ships through the maritime blockade lines. From 1 November 1914 until the summer of 1919, over 900 CRB-leased ships successfully navigated not only the British naval blockade but also German minefields and swarms of U-boats conducting unrestricted submarine warfare. By delivering essential food aid, the CRB helped the British government focus the full impact of the starvation blockade against Germany rather than against helpless neutrals in Belgium and Northern France.

Hoover's efforts were supported by the U.S. government. But the British also had to cooperate fully if this aid program was to work. Inspections of the CRB ships took place at Halifax, Canada. Beginning in August 1917, inspections of the cargoes could also be carried out during the loading process in U.S. harbors. This reform saved an estimated 30,000 tons cargo capacity by cutting the total number of transit days per month from 76 to only 60.[2] But some ships were still leaving from Halifax. On 6 December 1917, one of these CRB ships, the Norwegian-flagged ship SS *Imo*, reportedly exited the harbor on the wrong side of the passage, and rammed into the munitions

---

2 Ibid., citing Hoover to Auchincloss, 14 August 1917, CRB, Box 6, File 9, Hoover Institution Archives.

ship SS *Mont-Blanc*. The resulting explosion killed 1,782 people, and injured over 9,000. It also—conveniently from the U.S. point of view—destroyed the Royal Navy's main dockyards, thereby effectively destroying the main British-controlled naval port in North America. To Americans who were concerned about the British government using World War I to consolidate its control over Canada, this "accident" was a godsend.

Coincidentally, the very next day, on 7 December 1917, the U.S. Navy and the Royal Navy merged into one. This was an event fraught with tensions. In July 1917, Admiral John Jellicoe, the First Sea Lord, had requested a detachment of four American coal-burning dreadnoughts. Most U.S. Naval officers opposed giving Britain ships. Four long months passed before Admiral William S. Benson, who opposed this union, finally changed his mind. Between July and November 1917, he was subjected to constant lobbying by assistant chief of Naval Operations Captain William Veazie Pratt. Benson eventually capitulated. For the first time ever, American warships were integrated with the Royal Navy, the "legendary nemesis of the U.S. Navy."[3] Three days after Benson cabled Washington giving his approval, RADM Hugh Rodman assumed command of Battleship Division Nine. Wasting no time, Rodman led his four coal-burners to sea on 25 November. After an extremely rough passage, *New York*, *Florida*, *Delaware* and *Wyoming* steamed into the massive base of the British Grand Fleet in the roadstead of Scapa Flow in the Orkney Islands.

The date was 7 December 1917, just one day after the Halifax explosion. That day's "marriage" of American and British capital fleets lasted to the end of World War I in November 1918. Following a series of postwar disagreements the Anglo-American "vows" were renewed in 1939 and honored throughout World War II and the Cold War. This Anglo-American union has persisted to this day. Although there is no firm evidence that the American-leased *Imo* crashed into the *Mont-Blanc* on purpose, the virtual destruction of the Halifax naval dockyards just one day prior to this union guaranteed the British could not misuse these American ships against the United States. Was Halifax therefore "sacrificed" as a necessary precondition for this Anglo-American naval union? Or, to put it another way, if the Halifax explosion had not happened, would the naval union have failed to occur, thereby threatening the entire war effort?

---

3 Hagan and McMaster, "The Anglo-American Naval Checkmate."

Chapter 7

WOODROW WILSON'S CLERICAL ERROR AND THE MAY FOURTH MOVEMENT IN CHINA (1919)

Woodrow Wilson was wrongly blamed for betraying China at the 1919 Paris peace talks due to a chance clerical error. His "secret" compromise solution to the Sino-Japanese Shandong question divided the problem into "political" versus "economic" concerns. While fighting to return to China full control over all political rights, Wilson was willing to grant Japan the economic rights that Germany had previously held in the Shandong concessions, and which the Japanese government had acquired from Beijing by means of official—albeit secret—agreements. Wilson successfully negotiated this compromise with the Japanese delegation during the last week of April 1919, immediately prior to the announcement of the Paris Peace Conference's peace treaty. Coincidentally, Wilson's secretary back in Washington neglected to release this agreement, thereby helping to precipitate the 4 May 1919 student demonstrations in China that eventually resulted in the founding of the Chinese Communist Party.

President Wilson stood up for China's national sovereignty at the Paris Peace Conference ending World War I. On 29 April 1919, Wilson expressed his concerns that Japan might wrongly acquire Germany's former political rights—considered illegal by China—in Shandong province. He even went so far as to ask the Japanese envoy, Baron Makino, several detailed questions, first about underwater cables, then about railways and mines, to make sure that Japan was not being given more rights than Germany had previously enjoyed. Wilson was especially worried about Tokyo's contention that the Japanese citizens should enjoy extraterritorial rights along the railway lines in Shandong, warning the Japanese delegates that "He must say frankly that he could not do this. He asked the Japanese representatives to cooperate with him in finding a way out. He wanted to support the dignity of Japan, but he thought that Japan gained nothing by insisting on these leased rights being vested in the government." As for Japan's insistence on using Japanese police along the railways, Wilson clarified that "he did not mind Japan asking for these rights, but what he objected to was their imposing them."[1]

What Wilson hoped to do was convince Japan to forego its 21 Demands, signed in 1915 with ROC president Yuan Shikai, and develop its relations with China based on respect for China's sovereignty:

> President Wilson said that one of the worst features in [the] whole of these transactions had been the unfortunate 21 demands and these had included a demand for police instructors, although, of course, on a much wider basis. This had caused the greatest irritation, as it was an invasion of Chinese political and administrative independence. It was impossible to divorce transactions of this kind from the public impression they made. The present arrangement was, in public intimation, tied up with the impression made by the 21 demands. He admitted that the police point in itself was a minor one, but in its implications, both in China and the United States [...] it was very unfortunate.[2]

Wilson's proposal for circumventing the 21 Demands called for Japan to make a statement respecting China's sovereignty, and he recommended the following wording: "Surrender to China of all rights of sovereignty and retention with regard to the railway and the mines only of the economic rights of a concessionaire; to retain however privilege of establishing a non-exclusive settlement at Tsingtao [Qingdao]."[3]

After deliberation, the Japanese delegation agreed to Wilson's suggestion and on 30 April 1919 formally announced Japan's intended goals with regard to Shandong:[4]

> In reply to questions by President Wilson, Japanese delegate declared as follows: - the policy of Japan is to hand back the Shantung [Shandong] peninsula in full sovereignty of China, retaining only the economic privileges granted to Germany and the right to establish a settlement under the usual conditions at Tsingtao [Qingdao].

---

1 Bruce A. Elleman, *Wilson and China: A Revised History of the Shandong Question* (Armonk, NY: M.E. Sharpe, 2002), citing Japanese Ministry of Foreign Affairs Archive (Gaimushō), File: 2.3.1-3.4.
2 Ibid., citing Gaimushō, File: 2.3.1-3.4.
3 Ibid., citing Gaimushō, File: 2.3.1-3.1.
4 Ibid., citing Gaimushō, File: 2.3.1-3.1.

The White House,
Washington.

CODE

1 May, 1919.

The President of the United States,

Paris.

I have not made use of the Japanese statement, but am keeping my ear to the ground and waiting. My feeling is that an attempt to explain the compromise, when no demand is made, would weaken our position instead of strengthening it. I will therefore do nothing about the Japanese matter unless you insist. It would help if I could unofficially say: First. The date of your probable return to the country; Second. Whether tour country to discuss the League of Nations is possible. The adoption of the labor program as part of the peace program, is most important, but not enough emphasis is being placed upon it. Could you not make a statement of some kind that we could use here, showing the importance of this program as helping toward the stabilization of labor conditions throughout the world.

20633   TUMULTY.

Document 11: Tumulty's 1 May 1919 Cable to Woodrow Wilson

Document 2 Tumulty's 1 May 1919 cable to Woodrow Wilson.

The owners of the railway will use special police only to insure security for traffic. They will be used for no other purpose.

The police force will be composed of Chinese and such Japanese instructor[s] as the directors of the railway may select and will be appointed by the Chinese Government.

By phrasing Japan's position this way, Wilson convinced the Japanese delegation to retain certain economic rights in Shandong, but no military or political rights. Most importantly, this solution completely avoided referring back to, and thereby recognizing, the 1915 and 1918 Sino-Japanese agreements' infringement on China's sovereignty. In effect, Wilson convinced Japan to wipe the slate clean, and build all future Sino-Japanese diplomatic relations on the basis of equality and goodwill.

Wilson tried to find the best solution possible under the circumstances. But, coincidentally, Wilson's assistant back in Washington failed to publish this agreement in the local newspapers, as he had been instructed to do. Tumulty wrote: "I will therefore do nothing about the Japanese matter unless you insist." (See Document 2.) Since the Chinese did not realize a deal had been struck, and one that gave them most of what they wanted, the student demonstrations of 4 May 1919 were to turn China irrevocably away from Wilson and the West and toward socialism and eventually communism. When the Chinese Communist Party was later founded in July 1921, it was in part a reaction to China's misunderstanding of what had actually occurred in Paris.

Chapter 8

SOVIET GOLD MINING AND THE SUDDEN END TO THE MONGOLIAN GOLD RUSH (1924)

The USSR narrowly survived the 1920s and 1930s, perhaps surviving in part by tapping formerly unknown gold sources in Siberia and Outer Mongolia. An English-language letter dated 14 April 1924 from C. R. Bennett, a representative of an American banking consortium in China, to Wellington Koo, foreign minister of China, even warned him of a new German and Soviet consortium to mine gold in Outer Mongolia.[1] (See Map 3.) Coincidentally, Soviet political maneuvering in Outer Mongolia during fall 1924 strengthened the Soviet government's sphere of influence there, which allowed them to exploit these gold resources. Without access to these untapped gold riches, the Soviet government might have collapsed when the Great Depression hit unexpectedly in 1929.

After its 1921 invasion of Outer Mongolia, the Soviet government repeatedly promised China that it would withdraw its troops. But during May 1924, the American vice-consul in Kalgan, Edwin F. Stanton, reported that "the present Soviet Government, acting in an advisory capacity to the Mongolian Government, but actually dictating its policies and its administration, does not intend to relinquish either political or economic control of Outer Mongolia."[2] In fact, Moscow's creation of the Soviet bloc in 1924 to include Outer Mongolia has been ignored by most historians as insignificant. But the untapped Mongolian gold resources made it of great financial importance.

---

1 Bruce A. Elleman, *Diplomacy and Deception: The Secret History of Sino-Soviet Diplomatic Relations, 1917–1927* (Armonk, NY: M.E. Sharpe, 1997), 85–113 passim. Citing 14 April 1924, Wai-chiao Tang-an (WCTA), 03-32, 510(3).
2 Ibid., citing Alicia J. Campi, "The political relationship between the United States and outer Mongolia, 1915–1927: The Kalgan Consular Records," Indiana University Dissertation, 1988, 202–203.

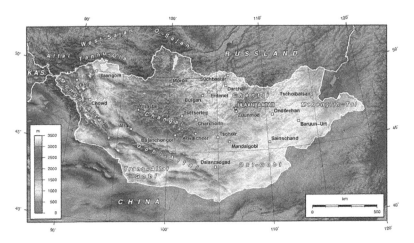

Map 3 Outer Mongolia or Mongolian People's Republic.

Even while publicly agreeing Outer Mongolia was part of China, the Soviet government sought to secretly retain it. Part of the mystery surrounding Soviet envoy Lev Karakhan's unwillingness to compromise on Outer Mongolia was cleared up during April 1924, when Koo received a communication from the Moore-Bennett company which directly related to the USSR's continued occupation of Outer Mongolia. This letter warned Koo that "[An] unimpeachable commercial source has reached me to the effect a composite political commercial financial technical group is now under establishment in Moscow and Berlin for the purpose of surveying and considering means of opening up and working all of the Eastern gold and other precious mineral fields of Siberia and particularly as affecting China's interest [...]"[3] This communication appears to have been the first detailed information that Koo received that the USSR and Germany were already cooperating with each other to exploit gold mines in Outer Mongolia.

The contents of this note are supported by documentary materials located in the Japanese Foreign Ministry Archives, which describe how a Councilor to the German Foreign Office, named Assmis, visited Outer Mongolia during 1922 on behalf of Count Brockdorff Rantzau. Assmis admitted that he was preparing for a conference in Moscow to determine "Russian and German interest[s] in developing the Far Eastern territories of Russia." Assmis also explained that "the Russian face has turned eastwards again,

---

3 Ibid., citing English-language letter from C.R. Bennett to Wellington Koo, 14 April 1924, WCTA, 03-32, 510(3).

and the Russians will take up the old [ts]arist imperialist policy against China and Japan," as well as proclaiming that Outer Mongolia "is practically on the way to be[ing] a Russian province."[4]

Koo's subsequent demand that Karakhan agree to abolish the USSR's 1921 treaty with Outer Mongolia, as well as withdraw all Soviet troops, would have directly interfered with this reported German-Soviet effort to exploit Outer Mongolia's natural resources. Even though the 31 May 1924 Sino-Soviet treaty agreed that Outer Mongolia was an integral part of China, it was becoming ever more clear that the Soviet government had other plans in mind. For example, after the death of the Bogdo Khan, the Living Buddha, on 20 May 1924, all lamas between 18 and 30 years old were drafted into the Mongolian army. This virtually eliminated organized religious opposition to the Soviet government's presence in Outer Mongolia.

In early September 1924, the last remaining American, European and Japanese businessmen were arrested and detained, reportedly as part of a purge within the Revolutionary Youth League, an organization "entirely dominated by Soviet Advisers and more particularly the head of the Secret Police."[5] By 14 September, these foreigners had been released, but their commercial activities ended as they were all forced to leave Outer Mongolia. The Soviet government's economic sphere of influence in Outer Mongolia was now complete.

The purge then underway also had important political ramifications. On 25 November 1924, Outer Mongolia promulgated a new constitution, changed its name to the Mongolian Peoples Republic, and renamed the capital from Urga to Ulaan Bataar. According to one scholar, it was this purge that allowed the Mongolia secret police to pave "the way for the complete Sovietization of Outer Mongolia."[6] Another has concluded that links between the USSR and Outer Mongolia soon became so close that beginning in 1925, "Stalinist restrictions, controls, and political radicalization unfolded in Mongolia with seeming inevitability, just as they were developing in the Soviet Union itself."[7]

Coincidentally, during the early 1920s, the Soviet government opened the Nalaikh gold mine just 20 miles from Ulaan Bataar. Over the next two decades, tons of gold were shipped out of Outer Mongolia to the USSR. These

---

4 Ibid., citing Gaimushō, File 2.5.1.106-1. Document # 437.
5 Ibid., citing Campi, 206.
6 Ibid., citing Peter S.H. Tang, *Russian and Soviet Policy in Manchuria and Outer Mongolia 1911–1932* (Durham: Duke University Press, 1959), 388–389.
7 Ibid., citing Robert Rupen, *How Mongolia Is Really Ruled: A Political History of the Mongolian People's Republic 1900–1978* (Stanford, CA: Stanford University Press, 1979), 44.

Mongolian gold reserves not only helped prop up the Soviet government during the Great Depression, but undoubtedly also helped the USSR win World War II. In 1945, Stalin defended the Soviet government's imperialist actions, citing Outer Mongolia's strategic importance.[8] But the rapacious nature of Moscow's foreign policy in Outer Mongolia was made especially clear after the success of the Chinese Communist revolution in 1949, when the USSR refused to open negotiations with the People's Republic of China (PRC) on the status of Outer Mongolia, and continued their opposition until the collapse of the USSR in 1991. In the meantime, billions of dollars of natural resources, including most importantly gold bullion, continued to be removed from Outer Mongolia. While the Nalaikh gold mine was closed down in the 1990s, at the time of writing it is estimated that over $1 trillion in gold and copper deposits remain in Mongolia, but all the trillions of dollars of easy-to-reach gold ore are long gone.

---

8 Ibid., citing Rupen, 45.

Chapter 9

THE SOVIET GREAT PURGES AND GULAGS AS A REACTION TO JAPAN'S PROPOSED IMMIGRATION POLICIES IN MANCHUKUO (1937)

Scholars of the Soviet Great Purges and the Siberian gulag (i.e., prison camp) system it produced have tended to emphasize only domestic factors that may have led to the Stalinist purges. But one highly coincidental foreign policy factor that deserves special attention was Tokyo's 1936 announcement that it intended to sponsor and pay for the trans-shipment of over 5 million Japanese immigrants to its puppet state of Manchukuo, which bordered on the USSR's Far Eastern territories. Even though Japan never even got close to carrying out this policy, since its program was voluntary only, by the end of World War II some five million transported European Russians were living in Siberia, many of them located right north of the Soviet border with Manchuria (see Map 4).

The history of Japanese immigration to Manchuria dates back to Japan's victory in the 1904–1905 Russo-Japanese war, when Japan obtained the southern branch of the Chinese Eastern Railway, which was renamed the South Manchuria Railway (SMR). In addition to the 170,000 Japanese who eventually worked directly for the SMR, thousands of other Japanese immigrants flocked to Manchuria during the following decades. According to Yosuke Matsuoka, the president of the SMR during the 1930s as well as Japan's foreign minister during World War II, Japanese immigration to Manchuria was considered to be the first line of defense against Russia, since the "leaders of Japan [...] suspected that defeated though she was, Czarist Russia would sooner or later strike back at the island Empire in revenge." Thus, the Japanese government decided that in Manchuria "encouragement might be offered for the settlement of as many Japanese as possible in the

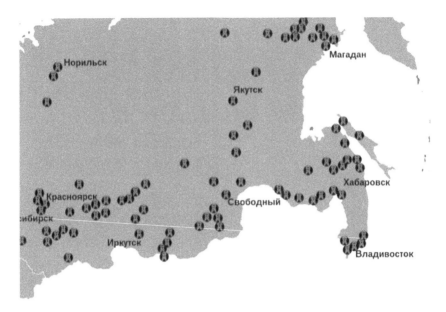

Map 4 Soviet gulags along the Sino-Manchurian border.

new land and for the launching of all sorts of enterprises by such settlers [...] indispensable to the protection of Japan's life-line of the Asiatic continent."[1]

After the 1931 "Manchuria Incident," when Japan invaded north-ern Manchuria, Japanese immigration increased dramatically. Between 1932 and 1936, the Tokyo Ministry of Overseas Affairs sponsored the migra-tion of approximately 3,000 Japanese settlers. But, during 1936, the Japanese government announced that during the next 20 years a total of 1,000,000 Japanese households, numbering about 5,000,000 people, would move to Manchukuo. During the first five years alone, some 100,000 families—approximately 500,000 people—would be settled in Manchukuo by the Manchuria Colonization Company, an organization established and funded by the Japanese government[2] (see Documents 3 and 4).

Not surprisingly, most of these Japanese immigrants were peasants. During 1937, about 6,000 families were expected to arrive, financed in part by a state subsidy of 1,300 yen per family. The primary reason given was that "the settlement of a large number of Japanese farmers in the new State will be

---

1 Yosuke Matsuoka, "The south Manchuria railway company: Its great mission and work," *Contemporary Manchuria*, Volume 1, No. 1 (April 1937), 1–14.
2 "An outline of Manchoukuo's second-stage construction program," *Contemporary Manchuria*, Volume 1, No. 3 (September 1937), 1–15.

Documents 3 and 4 Japanese announcement of Immigration Plan, 1 August 1936.

of great help in the preservation of her territorial integrity, since farmers in general are most attached to the land on which they live." Thus, the Japanese peasant emigrants in Manchukuo were vitally necessary "from the point of view of national defence inasmuch as Japan and Manchoukuo are so closely related geographically and otherwise that they are bound to stand and fall together."[3]

On 2 August 1937, Ambassador Uyeda and Manchukuo's prime minister Chang signed a final agreement to reorganize the Japanese-operated colonization company with the goal of becoming "the chief agency of settling Japanese farmers in Manchoukou, especially by acquiring and distributing lands and by providing the necessary financial assistance." This joint company was initially set up with 50,000,000 yuan working capital, provided

---

3 "The immigration of Japanese farmers to Manchoukuo: Its necessity and chances of success," *Contemporary Manchuria*, Volume 1, No. 3 (September 1937), 97–103.

equally by Japan and Manchukuo.[4] The mass movement of people as a military strategy is age-old. In 1937, one author supporting even greater Japanese immigration to Manchukuo concluded that although "it is needless to say that Manchukuo's territorial integrity is well preserved through the cooperation of Japanese and Manchukuo troops, the existence of a large number of Japanese farmers in Manchukuo will be of further aid in the strengthening of her national defence."[5]

Considering the long history of Soviet-Japanese friction, Moscow's response to the Japanese announcement that it was bringing five million immigrants to Manchukuo was predictable, especially when one considers that Tokyo had publicly declared that the vast majority of these immigrants would be established in new settlements close to Manchukuo's lengthy border with the USSR. Moscow, however, unlike Tokyo, which could use a wide range of economic incentives to entice its citizens to immigrate voluntarily, was simply in no position to offer comparable incentives to convince its citizens to move from European Russia to Siberia. Thus, the formation of a migration system based on forced labor camps—the infamous "gulag archipelago"—was arguably the only viable method available to Soviet officials for rapidly populating Siberia to meet the sudden threat of Japanese immigration.

Coincidentally, the USSR was also simultaneously building up the number of Soviet citizens on its side of the border. Since no sane European Russian would move to Siberia of their own free will, the Great Purges were initiated in September 1936 and continued through August 1938. During this period the number of European Russians living in gulags in Siberia quadrupled, from about 500,000 in 1934 to almost 2 million in 1938. In the end, Japan failed to convince 5,000,000 Japanese peasants to relocate willingly to Manchukuo. But by the end of World War II, there were almost exactly 5,000,000 Russians living in dozens of gulags throughout Siberia and on the Soviet side of the border with Manchuria.

---

4 "Reorganization of Manchuria colonization company," *Contemporary Manchuria*, Volume 1, No. 3 (September 1937), 110–111.
5 "The Immigration of Japanese Farmers to Manchoukuo," 97–103.

Chapter 10

SECRET WESTERN MANIPULATIONS BEHIND JAPAN'S PEARL HARBOR ATTACK (1941)

Contrary to popular wisdom, some politicians in the United States apparently wanted Japan to attack America, so that the U.S. government could join the war in Europe. During the 1930s, the U.S. strategy toward Japan evolved from "non-recognition of its invasion of Manchuria, to political neutrality, to trade embargo, to a combination of forward basing of the U.S. Fleet and trade cessation."[1] U.S. deterrence ultimately backfired, however, because the emperor chose a military strategy that had a remote hope of success over an even higher likelihood of regime change at home if Japan backed down after incurring such huge human and financial costs in China. Coincidentally, when Japan attacked Pearl Harbor, some American politicians celebrated, knowing that by this act the United States could now enter the war in Europe.

As Japan expanded its empire first into Manchuria (1931–33), then into North China (1934–36) and finally throughout Central and South China (1937–45), the U.S. government adopted a low-cost strategy starting with non-recognition. But Congress passed a succession of neutrality acts starting on 31 August 1935 that forbade trade with either side in a war. On 5 October 1937, Roosevelt's famous quarantine speech signaled the U.S. judgment that Germany and Japan were both pariah states. Thereafter, in mid-1938, the United States began escalating trade restrictions on the war materiel necessary for Japan to continue hostilities in combination with forward basing of the U.S. fleet at Hawaii starting in 1940.

Embargo seemed like a highly promising strategy, given Japan's overwhelming dependence on raw material imports for war materiel production. On 11 June 1938, in response to the many Chinese civilian deaths from the

---

1 S.C.M. Paine, "The allied embargo of Japan, 1939–1941: From rollback to deterrence to boomerang," in Elleman and Paine, *Navies and Soft Power*, 69–90, passim. Much of the description of the embargoes presented here is based on this chapter.

Japanese bombing of Guangzhou (Canton), Secretary of State Cordell Hull imposed a "moral embargo" on U.S. exports of aircraft and equipment. By June 1940, the U.S. government had instructed U.S. customs authorities not to permit certain equipment exports to Japan and on 2 July 1940, Congress passed the "Act to Expedite the Strengthening of National Defense" (the *Export Control Act*), which authorized the president to prohibit the export of war materiel and strategic resources in order to stockpile them at home.[2]

On 26 July 1940, on the first anniversary of the U.S. abrogation of its commercial treaty with Japan, Roosevelt cut the export to Japan of aviation gasoline and various categories of iron and steel scrap. Thereafter, the U.S. broadened the list of items embargoed. On 23 November 1940, the Council of Foreign Relations issued a confidential study on Japan's vulnerability to U.S. sanctions, warning that sanctions alone "would not necessarily stop her war machine."[3] Ignoring this warning, on 1 August 1941, Acting Secretary of State Sumner Welles revoked all valid licenses allowing the export of petroleum products to any country outside the Western Hemisphere, the British Empire, Egypt, the Dutch East Indies, unoccupied China and the Belgian Congo.[4] This meant no exports to Japan. Some believe that the oil embargo was not meant to be total, but a mistake resulting from a bureaucratic snafu.[5]

Japanese leaders interpreted the 1 August petroleum halt as a deadline for making alternate supply arrangements. Far from deterring Japan, these actions appear to have pushed Japanese leaders to put the finishing touches on their attack plans. Within a week of the total oil embargo, the Imperial Japanese Army favored going to war in the Pacific. At an Imperial Conference in September 1941, Prime Minister General Tōjō argued that together the U.S. oil embargo, its Lend-Lease aid to Russia and its increasing military aid to Chiang Kai-shek constituted an attempt to encircle and destroy Japan. War with the United States, on the other hand, offered a fifty-fifty chance of

---

2 Ibid., citing Richard L. Stokes, "Survey shows loss of U.S. war exports would cripple Japan," *Star*, 13 October 1940, Stanley K. Hornbeck Papers, Box 155, File "Embargo," Hoover Institution Archives.

3 Ibid., citing William Diebold, Jr., "Japan's vulnerability to American sanctions," *Studies of American Interest in the War and the Peace, Economic and Financial Series*, no. E-B 24, preliminary confidential memorandum first draft, 23 November 1940, 3, Stanley K. Hornbeck Papers, Box 369, File "Sanctions #2," Hoover Institution Archives; Irvin H. Anderson, Jr., "The 1941 De Facto Embargo on Oil to Japan," 212–214.

4 Ibid., citing Sumner Welles, Acting Secretary of State to the Collectors of Customs, 1 August 1941, FRUS, 1941, *The Far East*, vol. 4, 850.

5 Ibid., citing Irvin H. Anderson, Jr., "The 1941 De Facto Embargo on oil to Japan," 201–231.

Picture 5 Pearl Harbor attack.

Reminiscing about World War II, he recalled that on the night of Pearl
Harbor Winant and Harriman were both dining with him at his country place
at Chequers and had been listening to the "wireless" and had thought that
they had heard some dispatch about a bombing in the Pacific. But, he said,
"we weren't sure until the butler came in and told us definitely that Pearl
Harbor had been bombed." "And then," he said, "the most extraordinary
thing happened. Winant and Harriman got up and embraced each other and
danced around the room in delight." He said that he had learned later that
Winant had telephoned to Roosevelt and that Roosevelt had told him what a
serious situation it was but that Winant had insisted that it was a marvelous
thing. Churchill also said that he remembered well that General Marshall
had taken a much longer horseback ride on that day than had usually been the
case and that Bedell had not delivered a certain telegram." And he said:
"I would like to get Bedell to tell us about it." General Bedell Smith was
sitting across the room and he came over and Churchill took his arm and
said: "Tell us about that telegram that you didn't deliver on Pearl Harbor
Day," and Bedell said: "I won't talk about that."

Document 5 Excerpt from Churchill's diary on Pearl Harbor Day.

success. Within the fortnight, Japan attacked Pearl Harbor on 7 December
1941 (see Picture 5).

Coincidentally, rather than being met with widespread condemnation,
some American diplomats danced for joy at the news of the Japanese attack
(see Document 5). The average U.S. voter remained devoutly isolationist until
after the Japanese attack on Pearl Harbor. Following Japan's attack, however,
Germany conveniently declared war on the United States, which meant that
American forces were soon actively assisting England. This all suggests that
the 1 August 1941 petroleum embargo by Acting Secretary of State Sumner
Welles was perhaps no accident, but was meant all along as one way to get
America into the war in Europe.

Chapter 11

THE TRUE ORIGIN OF THE KAMIKAZES (1944)

Everybody just naturally assumes that Japan came up with the idea for the Kamikaze pilots. But coincidentally, in the Hollywood film *Flying Tigers* (1942), the co-pilot "Woody" convinces John Wayne to bail out of their plane and then—mortally wounded with a gunshot to the stomach—Woody flies the plane into a Japanese ammunition train, blowing it up. Even though Woody is dying it is a clear case of Kamikaze tactics, that is, using a plane as a flying bomb. Again, totally by chance, imprisoned Japanese diplomats being held at Greenbrier Hotel in West Virginia were shown recent Hollywood films. In 1943, the second U.S.-Japanese civilian exchange ship took place. One or more Japanese diplomats might have easily told friends, including Air Force friends, back in Tokyo about this Kamikaze scene in the Hollywood film. The Japanese, upon hearing this news, might have just as easily assumed that the film depicted a real military event, not fiction, and so adopted Kamikaze tactics themselves in retaliation.

After Japan's attack on Pearl Harbor, Japanese diplomats in Washington, D.C., and throughout the country were rounded up and sent to live at the Homestead Hotel in Hot Springs, Virginia. Some 785 Japanese diplomats and their families lived there from December 1941 through June 1942. Many of these diplomats were exchanged for detained U.S. citizens on the first exchange ship, *Gripsholm*, that left New York on 10 June 1942. Those that were not exchanged on the first ship were then moved to the nearby Greenbrier Hotel in West Virginia. It was a luxury resort hotel. The accommodations were considered top notch, and the foreign diplomats could enjoy shopping, swimming, playing tennis or playing board games.

Recent Hollywood movies were also shown to the guests. We know this because "Every day, bookkeepers and housekeepers, movie operators and telephone operators, painters and waiters, musicians and masseurs and others performed admirably under difficult conditions."[1] Even the regular Japanese-American relocation centers were well provided with films, and at Tule Lake there were three motion picture projectors for showing films in the mess halls, where: "Films are largely fairly recent Hollywood releases." In order to purchase a more modern film projector, $4,000 was expended by the Tule Lake Cooperative Enterprise and "plans are underway to have regular shows in the high school auditorium."[2]

On 8 October 1942, the John Wayne classic movie *Flying Tigers* premiered, introducing the character "Woody," played by actor John Carroll, who later served as the basis for the principal character by that same name in the Pixar animated film "Toy Story." As their damaged plane is going down, the co-pilot "Woody" convinces John Wayne to bail out, then—mortally wounded in the stomach—Woody intentionally flies the plane into a Japanese ammunition train, blowing it up. This was a classic wartime propaganda film about friendship and sacrifice, and was sure to have been a popular film at the Greenbrier Hotel. Some movie posters even show the attack on the munitions train (see Pictures 6 and 7).

The second exchange ship left on 2 September 1943. By this time, *Flying Tigers* had been out for almost an entire year. *Gripsholm* was carrying 1,330 Japanese nationals for a six-week voyage, including 61 from Canada and 31 from Mexico. After the exchange took place on 16 October 1943, the Japanese civilians made their way back to Japan. If only one of these 1,200 Japanese kept in American detention had seen *Flying Tigers* then upon their return to Japan they could have told the story of heroic Woody, the original American Kamikaze pilot. The first Japanese Kamikaze—meaning "spirit wind" and referring to the typhoons that stopped not one, but two, Mongol attacks of Japan—attacks took place on 25 October 1944, during the Battle of Leyte Gulf, just about exactly one year later.

The American military intensively studied Japanese military tactics. The U.S. Naval War College spent decades wargaming so as to prepare for war with Japan. Fleet Admiral Chester Nimitz famously commented that the U.S. Navy had, during the 1920s and 1930s, prepared for the Pacific war so effectively through planning, fleet problems and war college studies and games

---

1 Harvey Solomon, "When the Greenbrier and other Appalachian resorts became prisons for axis diplomats," 21 February 2020, www.smithsonianmag.com.

2 Bruce Elleman, *Japanese-American Civilian Prisoner Exchanges and Detention Camps, 1941–45* (New York: Routledge Press, 2006), passim. Citing Spanish Report on the Tule Lake Relocation Center entitled "Visit to Japanese Internees or Detainees," written by Antonio R-Martin on 24 September 1943 and dispatched to Japan on 2 November 1943 (No. 419); Gaimusho A700, 9-11-1-5-1.

Pictures 6 and 7 Movie posters for *Flying Tigers*.

that the only real surprise presented by the Japanese were the Kamikazes.[3] Perhaps this was because the idea for Kamikazes rests not with Japan but with Hollywood. Thus, strange as it might seem, this 1942 Hollywood make-believe *Flying Tigers'* scene lauding Woody's Kamikaze sacrifice might coincidentally be the original model for Japan's later Kamikaze attacks beginning in 1944.

3 Thomas C. Hone, with Trent Hone, "The Pacific War as one coherent campaign, 1941–1945," *International Journal of Naval History*, Volume 2 (August 2003). www.ijnhonline.org.

Chapter 12

WHY THE KURILE ISLANDS WERE DISPUTED AFTER WORLD WAR II

After World War II, the USSR occupied the two southernmost Kurile Islands, plus two of the Hobomai islands off Hokkaido. The Kurile Islands were considered strategically significant because Japan's naval fleet left from there to attack Pearl Harbor (see Map 5). Coincidentally, President Truman's Order No. 1 gave Stalin permission to occupy and hold parts of Japan "proper." By never signing a peace treaty, the modern-day Russian government still controls these four islands under the guise of occupying Japan "proper."

The Kurile chain consists of 36 islands stretching from the southern tip of the Kamchatka Peninsula to the northeastern edge of Hokkaido Island. The two most southern of these—Kunashiri and Etorofu (or in Russian: Kunashir and Iturup)—were traditionally thought by the Japanese to be part of Hokkaido Island. Through a series of nineteenth-century Russo-Japanese treaties, the Kuriles fell under the ownership of Japan: in the Treaty of Shimoda (1855) and the Treaty of St. Petersburg (1875), Japan handed over its interests in Sakhalin Island to Russia in return for total control of the Kurile Islands. Following the 1904–1905 Russo-Japanese War, the 5 September 1905 Portsmouth Peace Treaty allowed Japan to regain sovereignty over the southern half of Sakhalin. With the opening of Soviet-American negotiations for Soviet entry into the Pacific War, however, the centuries-old dispute over the Kurile Islands reemerged. Through a lengthy series of negotiations and agreements—including the Cairo Declaration, the Teheran Conference and the Yalta agreement—Stalin wove a diplomatic web that allowed the USSR to reoccupy the islands.

The October 1943 Cairo Conference, which the USSR did not attend, first raised the question of post-war territorial acquisitions. On 27 November 1943, the Allies issued the following declaration: "The three great Allies are fighting this war to restrain and punish the aggression of Japan. They covet no gain for themselves and have no thought of territorial expansion. It is their purpose that […] Japan will also be expelled from all other territories which

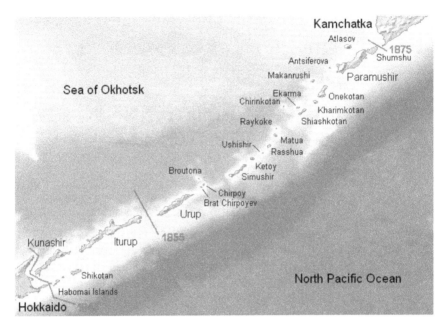

Map 5 The disputed Kurile Islands.

she has taken by violence and greed."[1] At the Teheran Conference, it has
been argued that President Franklin Roosevelt was persuaded that the Kurile
chain had been awarded to Japan in 1905, following the Russo-Japanese
War, and was receptive to Stalin's claim that both the Kuriles and southern
Sakhalin should become part of the USSR.[2]

Upon returning to Washington, Roosevelt informed the Pacific War
Council of Stalin's desires. Prior to the Yalta Conference, special committees
within the State Department prepared detailed memoranda concerning both
the Kuriles and Sakhalin. Professor George H. Blakeslee of Clark University
made three recommendations on the Kuriles: "(1) the southern Kuriles should
be retained by Japan subject to the principles of disarmament to be applied
to the entire Japanese Empire; (2) the northern and central Kuriles should
be placed under the projected international organization which should des-
ignate the Soviet Union as administering authority; and (3) in any case, the

1 United States, Department of State, *Foreign Relations of the United States, 1943, the
Conferences of Cairo and Teheran* (Washington: 1961), 448–449; hereafter FRUS.
2 Rosemary Hayes, *The Northern Territorial Issue* (Arlington, VA: Institute for Defense
Analyses, 1972), 6.

retention by Japan of fishing rights in the waters of the northern group should be given consideration."[3]

This memorandum was not included in the *Yalta Briefing Book*, however, and Roosevelt reportedly went to Yalta with his prior misconception unchanged.[4] On 11 February 1945, during the second day of meetings, Roosevelt held a closed session with Stalin and quickly concluded the fate of the Kuriles. The resulting agreement, signed by Stalin, Roosevelt and Churchill, appeared to support the USSR's claim to the entire island chain. It stated that "the Soviet Union shall enter into the war against Japan on the side of the Allies on condition that [...] the Kurile islands shall be handed over to the Soviet Union."[5]

Although historians have asserted that Roosevelt did not know which islands the term "Kurile" included, it is perhaps more significant that the Yalta agreement did not specify that "all" of the Kurile Islands would go to the USSR. This important point was left vague, perhaps because Roosevelt intended for the USSR to negotiate a new Kurile treaty with Japan to decide this very issue. In the absence of such a Soviet-Japanese agreement, however, Washington insisted that these disputed islands remained Japanese.

The State Department's interpretation of the Yalta agreement proves it did not believe the U.S. government had the authority to authorize such a Kurile transfer. This interpretation first became apparent after 15 August 1945, when Truman issued General Order No. 1 detailing the surrender of the Japanese Armed Forces. In this order, Truman did not specify to whom Japanese troops on the Kurile Islands would surrender, but mentioned only Manchuria, Korea, and Sakhalin: "The Senior Japanese Commanders and all ground, sea, air and auxiliary forces within Manchuria, Korea north of 38 degrees north latitude and Karafuto [Sakhalin] shall surrender to the Commander in Chief of Soviet Forces in the Far East."[6]

The next day, Stalin sent Truman an urgent message reminding him that according to Yalta "all the Kurile Islands" must be included in the region of surrender to Soviet troops. But Stalin also made a new demand that was

---

3 John J. Stephan, *The Kuril Islands: Russo-Japanese Frontier in the Pacific* (Oxford: Clarendon Press, 1974), 154, 240–245.

4 David Rees, *The Soviet Seizure of the Kuriles* (New York: Praeger Publishers, 1985), 61; quoting the memoirs of Charles Bohlen.

5 11 February 1945 copy of the Yalta Agreement, W. Averell Harriman collection, Library of Congress.

6 15 August 1945 copy of General Order Number 1 (document declassified on 20 August 1986), W. Averell Harriman collection, Library of Congress; Foreign Relations of the United States (FRUS), 1945, vol. 6, British Commonwealth and the Far East (Washington: 1969), 658–59.

never decided at Yalta: "To include in the region of surrender of the Japanese armed forces to Soviet troops the northern part of the island of Hokkaido [...] on the line leading from the city of Kushiro on the eastern coast of the island to the city Rumoe on the western coast of the island, including the named cities into the northern half of the island." Although Stalin called this demand "modest," Truman refused to consider Stalin's new demand that the Red Army should occupy northern Hokkaido. In an attempt to console Stalin, Truman did agree to allow a revised General Order No. 1 to state that Soviet troops could occupy the Kurile Islands: "The Senior Japanese commanders and all ground, sea, air and auxiliary forces within Manchuria, Korea north of 38 degrees north latitude, Karafuto [Sakhalin] and the Kurile Islands shall surrender to the Commander-in-Chief of Soviet Forces in the Far East."[7]

However, this revised General Order No. 1, issued on 19 August, still did not satisfy Stalin. On 22 August, Stalin informed Truman that "I and my colleagues did not expect [...] you [to] refuse to satisfy the request of the Soviet Union for the inclusion of the Northern part of the Island Hokkaido."[8] In a final attempt to placate Stalin, therefore, Truman agreed to revise General Order No. 1 for the third time. In its final form, this order read: "The senior Japanese commanders and all ground, sea, air, and auxiliary forces within Manchuria, Korea north of 38 degrees north latitude, Karafuto, and all of the Kurile Islands shall surrender to the Commander-in-Chief of Soviet Forces in the Far East."[9]

Truman undoubtedly hoped that by adding the word "all," he could dissuade Stalin from insisting on occupying northern Hokkaido. But his coincidental one-word revision was destined to have enormous consequences, since Stalin now claimed that the two southernmost islands in the Kurile Island chain—Kunashiri and Etorofu—had also been ceded to Russia, even though the Yalta agreement did not actually specify that these islands were part of the Kuriles. Soviet troops occupied Etorofu on 29 August 1945 and Kunashiri on 1 September 1945.

---

7 19 August 1945 copy of Washington's revision to General Order No. 1 (declassified on 21 August 1986), W. Averell Harriman collection, Library of Congress; FRUS does not reprint this document, which makes it difficult to see which concessions Truman made to Stalin, and in what order.

8 23 August 1945 copy of Stalin's 22 August 1945 letter to Truman (declassified on 21 August 1986), W. Averell Harriman collection, Library of Congress; FRUS, 1945, vol. 6, 687–88; undated final version of General Order No. 1, W. Averell Harriman collection, Library of Congress; FRUS does not include this document.

9 Rees, *The Soviet Seizure of the Kuriles*, 76–77.

Truman's change might make it appear that he ceded all of the Kurile Islands to Stalin, but what he really did was grant Stalin's 16 August request to allow Soviet forces to occupy "Japanese proper territory." On 27 August, Truman made it absolutely clear that Soviet troops occupied the Kuriles only temporarily and that they were not Soviet property. Truman concisely summarized the State Department's interpretation of the Yalta agreement when he told Stalin, "You evidently misunderstood my message [about the Kurile Islands] [. ...] I was not speaking about any territory of the Soviet Republic. I was speaking of the Kurile Islands, Japanese territory, disposition of which must be made at a peace settlement I was advised that my predecessor agreed to support in the peace settlement the Soviet acquisition of those islands."[10]

Truman's 27 August 1945 letter proves that General Order No. 1 did not hand over all the Kurile Islands to the USSR, but merely granted Soviet forces the right to occupy Kunashiri and Etorofu temporarily as part of Japan "proper." Truman's statement further disproves Soviet claims that they already held full sovereignty over the Kuriles. Only an official agreement between the USSR and Japan could transfer this sovereignty. Prior to the completion of any Russo-Japanese peace treaty transferring the Kuriles to the USSR, therefore, Washington has always argued that the islands remained Japanese territory.

---

10 27 August 1945 letter from Truman to Stalin (declassified on 21 August 1986), W. Averell Harriman collection, Library of Congress; FRUS, 1945, vol 6. The published document is an early draft from 25 August 1945, although the main points appear to be the same.

Chapter 13

HOW SECRET YALTA TALKS RESULTED IN POST-WAR SOVIET COLONIZATION (1945)

Stalin needed the support of the Allies to secure his victories in Eastern Europe and in Asia. During January 1945, Stalin promised to uphold the Yalta Conference's "Declaration on Liberated Europe," which guaranteed that open elections would be held in the Eastern European countries under his control. But Stalin quickly broke his promises in Europe, and in Asia too. For example, on 11 January 1943, the United States and Great Britain had completely eliminated all of their remaining extraterritorial rights and special privileges in China. But during the same year, Chiang Kai-shek for the first time confirmed that "the Sino-Soviet Agreement concluded on the basis of equality was not fully carried out."[1] Following the end of World War II, the Soviet government did not renegotiate its unequal treaties with China, but instead worked hand in hand with the Chinese communists to overthrow the Kuomintang. Stalin also consolidated Soviet control over Outer Mongolia.

Historians have previously attributed Chiang Kai-shek's 14 August 1945 decision to hold a plebiscite granting Outer Mongolia full independence from China to the 11 February 1945 Yalta agreement, in which Roosevelt, Churchill and Stalin decided: "The status quo in Outer-Mongolia (the Mongolian People's Republic) shall be preserved."[2] But when President Roosevelt agreed to support the *status quo* he never intended to push China into granting Outer Mongolia its independence. In fact, according to international law, the juridical *status quo* appeared to be based on the 31 May 1924 Sino-Soviet treaty, in which Moscow publicly recognized that Outer Mongolia was an integral part of China: "The Government of the Union

---

1 Chiang Kai-shek, *China's Destiny* (New York: The MacMillan Company, 1947), 143–144.
2 Edward R. Stettinius, Jr., *Roosevelt and the Russians* (Garden City, NY: Doubleday & Company, Inc., 1949), 351.

of Soviet Socialist Republics recognizes that Outer Mongolia is an integral part of the Republic of China and respects China's sovereignty therein."

But the true *status quo* was not what it appeared. China's sovereignty over Outer Mongolia was in fact undermined by a 31 May 1924 secret protocol with the USSR that recognized the 1915 tsarist tripartite treaty signed by Tsarist Russia, China and Outer Mongolia granting Outer Mongolia its autonomy from China. Although the 1924 protocol specified that the 1915 treaty was not to be enforced, Outer Mongolia's *de facto* autonomy was assured so long as Moscow refused to negotiate new terms. When Roosevelt promised to uphold the *status quo* at Yalta, therefore, he unwittingly provided Stalin with important leverage during secret Sino-Soviet negotiations that followed the Yalta Conference.

Minutes of these June–August 1945 Sino-Soviet talks indicate that Stalin relied on this alternative interpretation of *status quo* to demand that Chiang Kai-shek recognize Outer Mongolia's full independence from China.[3] Cornered by China's 1924 secret protocol, Chiang agreed, but only in return for Stalin's additional guarantee that the USSR "give to central Chinese Government alone all moral and material support."[4] These negotiating records provide compelling evidence that it was not Yalta but China's own secret diplomacy during the 1920s that forced Chiang to recognize Outer Mongolian independence as part of a final, and ultimately futile, attempt to halt Soviet aid to the Chinese Communists.

The widespread misunderstanding of what the Yalta agreement meant by *status quo* subsequently led one American scholar of Soviet history to conclude that *status quo* "implied Soviet domination of the area."[5] American scholars were quick to criticize President Roosevelt for this failing: "Roosevelt did not drive a hard bargain at Yalta."[6] The secrecy shrouding the 1924 protocol also led Taiwanese historians to blame Roosevelt for giving Stalin a "powerful pretext" for encroaching on Chinese national interests, mistakenly blaming Outer Mongolia's loss on Yalta's direct reference to the "Mongolian People's Republic."[7]

3 30 June 1945, "No. I. Meeting between Marshal Stalin and Dr. Soong," 3 pages, and 2 July 1945 - 14 August 1945, "Notes taken at Sino-Soviet Conferences," 76 pages, Victor Hoo Papers, Hoover Institution Archives (HIA).
4 2 July 1945 - 14 August 1945, "Notes taken at Sino-Soviet Conferences," 17.
5 George A. Lenson, "Yalta and the Far East," in John L. Snell ed., *The Meaning of Yalta* (Baton Rought: Louisiana State University Press, 1956), 157.
6 Immanuel C. Y. Hsü, *The Rise of Modern China* (New York: Oxford Press, 1990), 608.
7 Wu Hsiang-hsiang, *E-ti Ch'in-lueh Chung-kuo Shih* (A History of Imperial Russia's Invasion of China) (Taipei: Cheng Chung Book Company, 1954), 477; Lu Ch'iu-wen,

Dr. T. V. Soong, Chiang Kai-shek's brother-in-law and China's official envoy to Moscow during the 1945 Sino-Soviet negotiations, initially defended the American definition of *status quo* in his talks with Stalin:

> When I left Washington I had no idea that Outer Mongolia question would be a problem. I told Truman that we might settle this question by not discussing it. I said *status quo* was that juridical sovereignty remains with China. It is true we cannot exercise this sovereignty. Truman agreed and also Secretary of State. In Chungking I discussed with Chiang. None of us had any idea that Outer Mongolia would be an obstacle in our discussions.

Elsewhere, Soong repeated that the American and Chinese understanding of *status quo* did not mean Outer Mongolian independence: "That was not my understanding when I discussed [it] in Washington." Soong also explained why his government hesitated: "If we are to recognize *status quo* in Mongolia which has many times been recognized by Soviet Union as integral part of China our position as a government will be badly shaken before our people."[8]

China eventually backed down. But the pressure that Stalin could exert on Chiang came not from the Yalta agreement, but from the 1924 secret protocol recognizing Outer Mongolia's *de facto* autonomy from China. This protocol, when added to the USSR's absolute military control of Outer Mongolia and the Nationalists' military weakness, helps explain why Chiang was willing to use Outer Mongolian independence as a bargaining chip in his private negotiations with Stalin. In fact, Chiang Kai-shek sent a telegram on 9 July 1945, which stated, "Chinese government now willing make greatest sacrifice in the utmost sincerity to find fundamental solution of Chinese/Soviet relations" by agreeing to grant Outer Mongolia its independence in return for Soviet guarantees to uphold China's territorial integrity in Sinkiang and Manchuria, in addition to the following condition: "Because of Chinese communist administration and army, who are not united within the central government, wish Soviet Government to give to central Chinese Government alone all moral and material support. Any assistance given to China should be confined to the central government."[9]

Chung-e Wai-meng Chiao-she Shih-mo (The Ins and Outs of Sino-Russian Negotiations on Outer Mongolia) (Taipei: Cheng-wen Publishing Company, 1976), 242–247.

8 2 July 1945–14 August 1945, "Notes taken at Sino-Soviet Conferences," 13–16.

9 Ibid., 17–18.

Thereafter, in the Sino-Soviet treaty of friendship and alliance signed on 14 August 1945, Molotov included the following note: "In accordance with the spirit of the aforementioned treaty, and in order to put into effect its aims and purposes, the Government of the USSR agrees to render to China moral support and aid in military supplies and other material resources, such support and aid to be entirely given to the National Government as the Central Government of China."[10] These conditions prove that Chiang agreed to recognize Outer Mongolia's independence only in exchange for Stalin's promise not to support the Communists in their struggle against China's Nationalist government.

Coincidentally, Outer Mongolia has always been portrayed by the USSR and China as a separate independent country. But the minutes of the Sino-Soviet negotiations indicate that this portrayal was merely a means to protect China's national honor, in other words, a way to save China from "losing face." To preserve China's dignity, it was Chiang Kai-shek who suggested holding a fake plebiscite in Outer Mongolia. Chinese and Soviet government officials exchanged notes during August 1945 providing for a plebiscite in Outer Mongolia, after which China promised to recognize Outer Mongolia's independence. This plebiscite was merely for form's sake, however, which helps explain why China did not dispute the results when it was later reported that 98.14% of Outer Mongolia's electorate, many of them nomadic herdsmen, voted in the hastily arranged plebiscite, all of them for independence.[11] The Nationalist government thereafter officially recognized Outer Mongolia's complete independence from China on 1 January 1946.

---

10 31 January 1952, "Statement by United States Delegate John Sherman Cooper in the Political Committee of the United Nations General Assembly in the Discussion of Threats to the Political Independence and Territorial Integrity of China, at Paris, France, January 28, 1952." Maxwell Hamilton collection, HIA, Box #1.
11 Max Beloff, *Soviet Far Eastern Policy Since Yalta* (New York: Institute of Pacific Relations, 1950), 9.

Chapter 14

SECRET NEGOTIATIONS OF THE SINO-SOVIET BORDER (1945)

By early August 1945, only one major Sino-Soviet issue was left unresolved, a detailed agreement as to where exactly the Sino-Soviet boundary ran. With Japan's surrender imminent, it was important to Chiang Kai-shek that the agreement on Outer Mongolia be announced soon, so that the Chinese people could be convinced that Outer Mongolia's loss was a necessity of war. On 11 July 1945, Soong expressed his concern that the joint Sino-Soviet declaration on Outer Mongolia not mention the border, since there were still many disagreements about the disposition of the boundary line. Stalin agreed, suggesting that they retain the "*status quo*," but Soong retorted: "These is dispute about *status quo*."[1] Negotiations were broken off after 12 July, so that Stalin and Molotov could attend the conference at Potsdam, but talks resumed once again on 7 August. Coincidentally, during this almost four-week break, the Chinese envoy T. V. Soong had the opportunity to travel back to Chungking to consult personally with his brother-in-law Chiang Kai-shek. Based on Chiang's decisions, the final points of the upcoming Sino-Soviet declaration were determined between 7 and 14 August 1945.

The issue of Outer Mongolia's borders with China was of great importance to Soong. After returning from Chungking, he presented two maps to Stalin, one Russian and one Chinese, which outlined the Sino-Mongolian border. The following exchange then took place:

Soong: We would like to come to agreement on Outer Mongolia before we recognize independence: frontiers.
Stalin: We decided within existing boundaries.
Soong: We did not agree on anything concrete as I had no map.
Stalin: We did not mention boundaries.

---

1 2 July 1945–14 August 1945, "Notes taken at Sino-Soviet Conferences," 31.

Soong: We must recognize something and settle boundary so as to avoid friction.
Stalin: O.K.

But, on 10 August, Stalin disputed the maps which Soong had presented: "Re frontiers Chinese map is not well founded. Existing frontiers should be recognized."[2]

Stalin stuck to this proposal because the existing borders actually included extensive Manchurian territories which Tokyo had secretly ceded to Moscow during Outer Mongolia-Manchukuo border negotiations in the 1930s. Stalin clearly hoped to retain the largest amount of Chinese territory possible. The Chinese delegation, on the other hand, pleaded with Stalin to define the border between Outer Mongolia and China, even suggesting that the two countries use a Chinese college atlas as their guide. But Stalin advocated that the current borders be respected:

> Frontiers existing for 26 years was established without any disputes with China. Our topographers went there and drew on map a line which separated Chinese and Mongolian guards. That's west and south. Re east there were disputes with Japanese. Then there was an agreement concluded. If we re-examine, it will take time, certain pieces will be taken, others given. Your Russian map is not valid.

After an intense debate, the Chinese delegation insisted that all they wanted was "clarity," and: "We want to know where the line is." But, Stalin was determined not to discuss the border, pointing out that China had never challenged the border before, to which Soong replied: "We always considered Outer Mongolia as Chinese and there was no need to challenge."[3]

Stalin was aided enormously by the fact that negotiations were under a time limit, since once Japan surrendered it would become more difficult to convince the Chinese people that the Nationalists' concessions were necessary. On 13 August 1945, Soong backed down, therefore, and resolved the issue of borders in a haphazard fashion: "Chiang wanted agree on boundaries first, but Stalin said it would take too much time. So Chiang accepts existing boundaries. That question is therefore excluded from questions to be settled." With Soong's concession, not only did Stalin gain China's official recognition of the USSR's long-standing hold over Outer Mongolia, but

2 Ibid., 47–49.
3 Ibid., 53–54.

the expanded borders, which the Soviets had formerly negotiated with Japan during the 1930s, remained unchanged, all in return for Stalin's empty promise to support only Chiang Kai-shek and the Nationalists.[4]

After the formation of the PRC on 1 October 1949, Outer Mongolian independence continued over the protests of the Communists, who felt that Outer Mongolia had previously been promised to them. Soviet leaders adamantly refused to reopen border negotiations with China, a dispute that continued to plague Sino-Soviet relations during the following decades.[5] The USSR arguably acquired an estimated 600,000 square miles of territory from China. This diplomatic victory rivaled the heyday of tsarist Russia's nineteenth-century territorial expansion, when China ceded approximately 665,000 square miles of territory to Russia.[6] Without Outer Mongolia, the amount of territory secured by Russia was approximately five times the area of Japan and more than seven times that of Great Britain; including Outer Mongolia, this territory exceeded that of India and was more than one-third the size of the United States[7] (see Map 6).

Sino-Soviet negotiating records from 1945 confirm that the USSR resorted to secret diplomacy to complete the tsarist plan of separating Outer Mongolia from China, a plan that dates to the 1850s, but was put into action in 1912. These diplomatic records prove that Russia's foreign policy in Outer Mongolia remained constant from 1912 through 1945. Coincidentally, when Soong returned to China to discuss the location of the Sino-Soviet border with Chiang Kai-shek, it turned out Chiang was willing to negotiate away China's border disputes in return for Stalin's promise of support. All such promises proved empty, however. In the end, Soviet expansionism was simply the most recent stage in the long tradition of Russian imperialism.

---

4 Ibid., 70.
5 1 August 1964, "An Interview with Chou En-lai," Dennis J. Doolin, *Territorial Claims in the Sino-Soviet Conflict* (Stanford, CA: Hoover Institution Studies: 7, 1965), 45.
6 Alan J. Day, ed., *Border and Territorial Disputes*, Keesings Reference Publication (Detroit: Gale Research Co., 1982), 259–261.
7 *The New Encyclopaedia Britannica*, vol. 10, 34; vol. 18, 864; vol. 9, 276; vol. 18, 905.

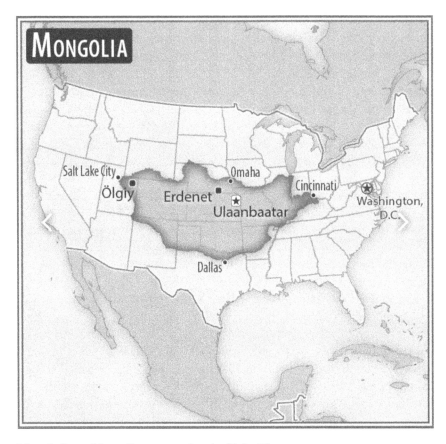

Map 6 Outer Mongolia compared to the United States.

Chapter 15

THE CIA ARGUMENT FOR WHY CHINA SHOULD BE ALLOWED TO BECOME COMMUNIST (1948)

Most people assume that after World War II the U.S. government made a mistake not fighting in China against the communists. But the U.S. government's main goal was to try to break up the Sino-Soviet alliance. A secret CIA report from December 1948 even advised letting the Chinese communists dominate all of the mainland of China in order to accelerate this split. Once the communists succeeded in taking all of the mainland, it was necessary to make Mao Zedong as dependent on Russia as possible, so as to increase tensions. Prior to Mao's visit to Moscow in early 1950, therefore, the U.S. government refused to recognize Beijing, which meant "the Chinese Communists cannot now play off one great power against another, since they have no non-Soviet allies at the moment."[1] It also put extreme pressure on China by establishing the Taiwan Strait Patrol in 1950 and adopting a strategic embargo on Chinese imports.

We now know that the USSR actively intervened in the Chinese Civil War against Chiang Kai-shek and on the side of Mao Zedong and the communists. Sino-Soviet tensions were already on the rise, however, even before Mao's proclaimed victory on 1 October 1949. In August 1948, British officials were reporting that Russian officials in Dairen had begun to exclude not just Nationalist forces from the port facilities, but also "the armed forces of the Chinese Communists."[2] Coincidentally, right after this British report came out, the CIA submitted its own report in December 1948 that recommended the Chinese communists be allowed to dominate all of the mainland of China, without U.S. opposition, since there would probably be "no chance

---

1 Summary of Telegrams, Top Secret, 27 November 1949, Harry S. Truman Presidential Library (HSTPL).
2 Letter from British Embassy in Nanking to Foreign Office, 13 August 1948, WO 208 4571, British National Archives.

economic situation in North and Central China to the point where any Communist program appears more desirable to the people than a Nationalist survival.

A Communist-dominated government will probably come to power as a result of what is in effect the surrender of the National Government. This government will prob-ably be proclaimed as a "coalition," and it will include many non-Communists, among them members of the present National Government. As a "coalition" it will have the advantage of not necessarily forfeiting international recognition. It is almost certain, however, that Communist officials will dictate the policies of such a government.

There is no doubt that the Chinese Communist Party has been and is an instru-ment of Soviet policy. While there is no guarantee that the USSR will always find the Chinese Communists dependable, there appears to be no chance of a split within the Party or between the Party and the USSR until the time of Communist domination of China.

Note: The information in this report is as of 1 December 1948.
      The intelligence organizations of the Departments of State, Army, Navy, and the Air Force have concurred in this report.

Document 6 CIA Report on the communists taking all of mainland China.

of a split within the Party or between the Party and the USSR," until after the "Communist domination of China"[3] (see Document 6).

With the beginning of the Korean conflict in 1950, the U.S. furthermore adopted a "sea denial" strategy, sending the Seventh Fleet into the Taiwan Strait to stop a planned PRC invasion of Taiwan. Fear of communist expan-sion along the first island chain led the U.S. government to support Taipei during the two Taiwan Strait crises in 1954–55 and 1958. Washington also felt obliged to sign security treaties supporting Chiang Kai-shek's efforts to defend a number of offshore islands from PRC attack.

Meanwhile, Sino-Soviet tensions were on the rise. According to a 1952 agreement, all Soviet military forces were scheduled to withdraw from the Manchurian ports by 31 May 1955. Moscow also agreed to transfer "the installations in the area of the Port Arthur [Lüshun] naval base to the Government of the People's Republic of China." When Moscow said it would return the various Manchurian railways and the Lüshun naval base to China without charge, Mao evidently thought that the USSR would also leave the large caliber guns that were protecting the port. But at the last minute the First Secretary of the Communist Party of the USSR, Nikita Khrushchev,

---

3 Central Intelligence Agency, "Chinese Communist Capabilities for Control of all China," Secret, 10 December 1948, HSTPL.

refused to transfer the artillery protecting this strategic base from attack by sea. Instead, Khrushchev demanded that China must pay for the full price of these guns: "These are very expensive weapons, we would be selling them at reduced prices."[4]

Moscow's decision during spring 1955 to strip the Port Arthur naval base of its main defensive weapons left China highly vulnerable in Manchuria, since the history of the Sino-Japanese War of 1894–95 and the Russo-Japanese War of 1904–05 had shown that naval invasions could easily reduce these bases from the sea. This Russian decision to not give Chinese these advanced weapons was perhaps intentional. During May 1955, Dulles even told Molotov during meetings in Vienna that "we had obtained from the Chinese Nationalists arrangements which we thought would enable us to influence the situation for peace from our side and he suggested that the Soviet Union could do the same with the Chinese Communists," in particular since "the Chinese Communists were dependent upon Russia for various strategic supplies and planes and could not develop their plans without Russian support."[5]

Khrushchev's decision not to leave the port defenses intact was a clear sign that the USSR was unwilling to back Mao's offensive to retake the offshore islands. He further hinted that the USSR's nuclear umbrella might not cover the Taiwan Strait. During 1958, Khrushchev, in what proved to be a vain attempt to convince Mao of the value of retaining the floundering Sino-Soviet naval coalition, reminded him: "On the issue of Port Arthur [...] it was advantageous for you that the Soviet Army was in Port Arthur and Manchuria."[6] But in the long run, the USSR's exclusionist tactics, which had been extremely successful during the late 1940s against the Nationalists, proved to be a double-edged sword that eventually undermined the foundations of the Sino-Soviet alliance. By the late 1950s, this policy had resulted in the Sino-Soviet rift.

As Nationalist rule imploded in China in the late 1940s, President Truman decided it was not worth billions of dollars and millions of men defending Nationalist China. U.S. military advisers in China were "unanimous in the view that short of the actual employment of US troops in China no amount of military assistance can now save the Chiang Kai-shek regime in the face

4 Nikita Sergeevich Khrushchev, Sergei Khrushchev, *Memoirs of Nikita Khrushchev: Statesman, 1953–1964* (College Park: Penn State Press, 2007), 434.
5 Conversation at Ambassador's Residence, Vienna on May 14, 1955, TOP SECRET, 17 May 1955, Dwight D. Eisenhower (DDE) Subject Series Box 70, State, Dept. of (May 1955), 2, Dwight D. Eisenhower Presidential Library (DDEPL).
6 *Cold War International History Project Bulletin*, Issue 12/13 (Fall/Winter 2001), 254–255.

of the present political, military and economic deterioration."[7] Truman's goal was instead to push the USSR and China closer together, with the ultimate goal of breaking them apart.

As early as 2 January 1950, Truman was told that the Chinese would never follow the "Moscow line" because the "Chinese are not built that way." Furthermore, due to the potency of the "Asia for the Asiatics" movement, the Russians were "not accepted by Orientals as Asiatics."[8] Pushing the two countries into working together eventually tore them apart. On 25 September 1952, Republican Senator Lehman even admitted that China "could have been saved, if at all, [only] by all-out military intervention on our part." Not only would the U.S. have "become bogged down in the immense expanse of China, in a war to keep Chiang-Kai-Shek in power, [but it] [...] would have cost us millions of men and billions of dollars."[9] Rather than being a failed policy, therefore, the U.S. government's decision to let Mao Zedong and the communists take all of mainland China was a huge strategic success. Over time, political tensions eventually resulted in the Sino-Soviet split during the late 1950s, just as the CIA had predicted would happen a decade before in December 1948.

7 Summary of Telegrams, TOP SECRET, 8 November 1948, Papers of Harry S. Truman (PHST), SMOF-Naval Aide, Box 23, State Department Briefs File, HSTPL.
8 Letter from H.T. Goodier to Harry S. Truman, 2 January 1950, PHST, Official File, OF 150-G, Box 761, Formosa, HSTPL; underlining in the original.
9 Letter from Guy Carolin to Harry S. Truman, 26 September 1952, PHST, Official File, OF 150, Box 760, File O.F. 150 Misc. (1951-53) [1 of 2], HSTPL.

Chapter 16

BOTH NORTH VIETNAMESE TONKIN GULF ATTACKS WERE PERHAPS REAL (1964)

One of the major events that historians use to date the beginning of the U.S. involvement in the war in Vietnam is the Gulf of Tonkin Resolution, signed on 10 August 1964. This resolution was proposed by President Johnson on 5 August 1964 after two North Vietnamese attacks on U.S. Navy ships, one on 2 August 1964 and the other two days later on 4 August 1964 (see Map 7). While the first encounter was well-documented, the North Vietnamese denied the second attack ever took place. In 2005, a National Security Agency study from the time was declassified that cast doubt on the second attack. But, coincidentally, several declassified documents held at the Lyndon Baines Johnson Presidential Library in Austin, Texas, now appear to show that the second attack really did happen.

American participation in the Vietnam War began in early August 1964, when the Congress approved a Southeast Asia Resolution by a vote of 88 to 2 in the Senate and 416 to 0 in the House of Representatives. On 10 August 1964, President Johnson signed into law the Gulf of Tonkin Resolution. By this action, Congress "approves and supports the determination of the President, as Commander in Chief, to take all necessary measures to repel any armed attack against the forces of the United States and to prevent further aggression." Critics of this resolution have since argued that while the first attack on 2 August 1964 was undoubtedly valid, the second attack on 4 August was not, which makes the resolution's wording suspect: "Whereas naval units of the Communist regime in Vietnam, in violation of the principles of the United Nations and of international law, have deliberately and repeatedly attacked United States naval vessels lawfully present in international waters […]"

The first attack occurred on 2 August 1964 when three North Vietnamese torpedo boats attacked the USS *Maddox*. This U.S. Navy destroyer was cruising in the Gulf of Tonkin in waters claimed by North Vietnam as within its

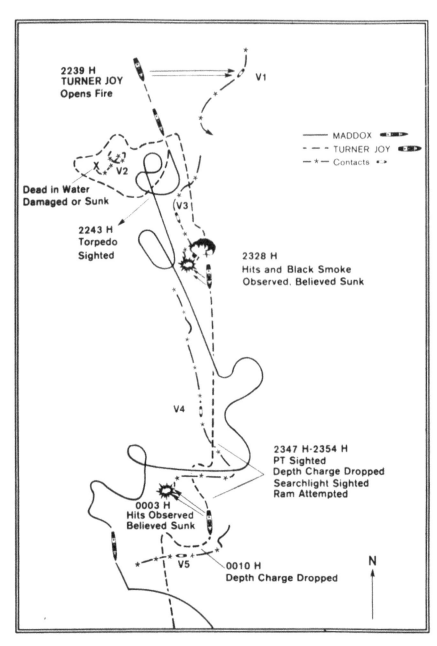

Map 7 Tonkin Gulf incident.

12-mile line of control, a claim not recognized by the U.S. government at the time which only recognized 3 nautical miles. After returning fire and expending six torpedoes of its own, all misses, *Maddox* left the engagement undamaged. Four Navy F-8 Crusader jets followed the North Vietnamese torpedo boats and damaged all three of them. While this attack was serious enough that President Johnson could have responded then, it was thought that another future incident might be even more unequivocal.

This apparently happened just two days later on 4 August 1964, when *Maddox* and *Turner Joy* returned to the area to continue their patrol, this time cruising about 8 miles off North Vietnam's shores. The attack occurred just after midnight at Lat 18-17N Long 107-32E. A "Secret" report (later declassified on 20 April 1976) from 4 August entitled "Sitrep No 2 Gulf of Tonkin Action" claimed that "two PTs sunk, two damaged, *Turner Joy* reports tracking two sets of radar contacts and firing on thirteen." This early report ended, however, by stating that the "sequence of events" was "still not entirely clear at the moment."[1]

The next "Secret" report at the Johnson Library was dated 6 August. By this time, Johnson had already submitted his Tonkin resolution to Congress. It is doubtful that anybody paid too much attention to these additional reports at the time. But it stated: "Consider proof of attack substantiated by 3 sightings described below." The first piece of evidence was a torpedo sighted by Jerome John, Larry Litton and Edwin Sentenel. After *Maddox* reported a torpedo from the direction of the initial contacts, "*Turner Joy* maneuvered to avoid" and the torpedo was observed 300 feet off the port side "on exactly the course (bearing) reported by Maddox." When a searchlight was used it reportedly showed a torpedo boat silhouette and Donald Sharkey, Kenneth Garrison, Delner Jones, and Arthur Anderson did the following: "When asked sketch boat they accurately sketched P4 type PT boat including lack of Radome, none had ever seen a picture of a P4 before."[2]

A bit later a fuller report was submitted. In it, Matthew Allasre and David Prouty signed the following statement: "On the night of Aug 4 during the engagement I was manning a thirty claibre (*sic*) machine gun on the platform behind the signal bridge. 13 different occasions during the action I saw a light pass up the port side of the ship go out ahead and pass down the starboard side. I believe this to be one or more small boats going at high speed." This

---

1 "Sitrep No 2 Gulf of Tonkin Action," 4 August 1964, SECRET, declassified on 20 April 1976, Lyndon Baines Johnson Presidential Library (LBJPL).
2 "Proof of Attack (U)," 6 August 1964, SECRET, declassified on 15 April 1977, LBJPL.

was corroborated by Jose San Augustine: "On the night of August 4 during the engagement I was stationed on the thirty caliber aft of the signal bridge. I saw the outline of a boat which was silhouted [sic] by the 3 inch projectile bursts when we were firing at it."[3]

Other sailors made similar statements, such as R. B. Corsette swearing his Mark Director 51 gun picked up several contacts, but then he lost them when "the ship began maneuvering erratically to evade torpedoes." Kieth Pane testified that his Mark 56 Director locked in on two targets and that his "Director tracked the target on a steady bearing with a slight decrease in range indicating approximately a parallel course and speed." Meanwhile, Captain John Herrick reported that in the CIC of *Maddox* he witnessed tracking of "approximately 5 contacts lying in wait." At some point "torpedo noises were picked up by the ships sonar," which caused *Maddox* to adopt a "weaving course" to avoid the torpedoes. Although a bit less certain that they were under attack, Frederick Frick stated, "CIC net indicated that *Turner Joy* had lockons on definite targets," and he concluded: "I firmly believe that torpedo attacks were conducted on *Maddox* and *Turner Joy* vic 18-38N 107-2 4E at high speed (40 plus kts) craft commencing at 2154I 4 August 1964." Finally, Commander H. L. Ogier testified "I am now convinced that the torpedo attacks did take place."[4]

Perhaps still not sure that a second North Vietnamese attack had taken place, a Top Secret report (declassified on 11 April 1977) was entitled "Verification Proof of Attack." In it, the testimony of around a dozen pilots who witnessed the action were compiled. G. H. Edmondson and J. A. Barton stated that they saw "gun flashes on the surface of the water and bursting light AA at their approximate flight altitude." When flying about one-and-a-half miles ahead of the American destroyers Edmondson testified he saw a "snaky" high-speed wake. Barton also reported he saw a "dark object in the wake of the leading destroyer approximately midway between the two ships," which "confirms sighting reported shortly before by the controlling destroyer."[5]

By the time this final "verification proof of attack" report arrived on 7 August it hardly mattered, since Congress had already passed the resolution on 7 August 1964. Once Johnson signed the bill on 10 August 1964, he was

---

3 "Night Engagement 4 August 1964," 6 August 1964, SECRET, declassified on 15 April 1977, LBJPL.

4 Ibid.

5 "Verification Proof of Attack," 7 August 1964, TOP SECRET, declassified on 11 April 1977, LBJPL.

pre-authorized by Congress to do whatever was necessary to assist "any member or protocol state of the Southeast Asia Collective Defense Treaty." Still, the largely coincidental declassification in 1976–77 of so many reports providing signed testimony to a second attack on 4 August 1964 would appear to undermine those critics who have called the reports of a second attack the "Tonkin Gulf Lie."[6]

---

6 Jeff Cohen and Norman Solomon, "30-Year Anniversary: Tonkin Gulf Lie Launched Vietnam war," 27 July 1994, *Fair*, www.fair.org.

Chapter 17

THE U.S. ANTI-SOVIET BLOCKADE DURING THE VIETNAM WAR (1965)

According to Gordan Chang, President Eisenhower's top priority was to break apart the Sino-Soviet monolith, so in his 1963 memoir *The White House Years* he barely mentioned Sino-Soviet tensions, so as "to avoid saying anything that could hinder the emergence of the Sino-Soviet split."[1] Under President Johnson, the split in the Communist bloc gradually deepened. A Top Secret CIA report from 22 February 1965 cited an unnamed Soviet source as saying "that Kosygin's trip to Hanoi will result in the Soviets giving 'defensive' aid to North Vietnam in the form of fighter planes, SAMs and radar equipment."[2] The CIA reported that on 28 March 1965, a three-way agreement among the USSR, China and North Vietnam had been reached to transport arms shipments across China by railway. Coincidentally, a declassified report of a sunken Soviet cargo ship carrying missiles to North Vietnam might explain why these Surface-to-Air Missiles (SAMs) had to be brought by railway through China (see Document 7).

Transporting missiles by train required China's cooperation. Beginning in 1965 the Soviet government felt obliged to provide North Vietnam with SAMs. The first SAM site was spotted from the air on 5 April 1965, located 15 miles southeast of Hanoi, but there were as yet no missile equipment there. However, this did not "mean the end of Sino-Soviet friction on this issue." In particular: "Moscow has shown itself reluctant to date to ship extensive aid to North Vietnam by sea, and recent Soviet allusions to an 'American blockade' suggest that the USSR fears a repetition of Khrushchev's disastrous backdown in the face of the US naval quarantine in the Cuban Missile

---

1 Gordan H. Chang, *Friends and Enemies: The United States, China, and the Soviet Union, 1948–1972* (Stanford: Stanford University Press, 1990), 331 n24.
2 CIA Memorandum, "The Situation in Vietnam," Top Secret Dinar/Declassified with Redactions 7/22/1999, 22 February 1965, Box 49, Folder 3, Document 28a, National Security File, Country File, Vietnam, LBJPL.

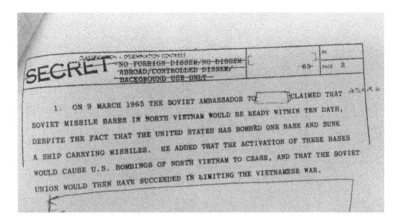

Document 7 Secret report of Soviet ship sinking.

Crisis. Since both air and land transit of significant quantities of Soviet military aid to the DRV would almost certainly necessitate passage over or through China, there remain ample opportunities for further difficulties and mutual recriminations." In fact, China was placing strict limits on the transit of Soviet personnel, and Presidium Member Suslov said that "although the Chinese had agreed to let Soviet nationals go through China by rail, they had 'changed their minds several times in this regard'."[3]

It was hoped that U.S. military pressure would provide "real inhibitions upon adventures by Peking in Hanoi in Southeast Asia." On 27 April 1965, the CIA predicted in a Secret memo that the Soviet government felt "unable to bear passively the opprobrium which the Chinese are only too ready to heep upon them for abandoning the struggle in Vietnam." As a result, the post-Khrushchev leadership "feels compelled to act, even in the face of risks which Khrushchev had turned away from."[4]

When assessing the possible impact of using B52 bombers against North Vietnam's fighter planes, bombers, and SAM sites, on 2 June 1965 the CIA concluded that "The Soviets would almost certainly feel compelled to comply promptly with DRV requests to provide substitutes for those weapons systems destroyed by the US attack, though they might not again provide bomber aircraft." Their estimate that "the Soviets would probably conclude that

---

3 CIA Memorandum, "Status of Soviet Military Assistance to North Vietnam," Top Secret/Declassified with Redactions 11/24/1981, 15 March 1965, Box 49, Folder 4, Document 5, National Security File, Country File, Vietnam, LBJPL.

4 CIA Memorandum, "Future Soviet Moves in Vietnam," 27 April 1965, Box 16, Folder 3, Document 99, National Security File, Country File, Vietnam, LBJPL.

they had little choice but to increase aid to the DRV" was accurate.[5] Clearly, Moscow felt trapped by its commitments to North Vietnam to provide unlimited numbers of SAMs.

Soviet officials promised to provide North Vietnam with adequate weapons. But on 2 April 1965, the CIA confirmed that no arms had been transported to North Vietnam by sea: "Evidence to date has not indicated deliveries, past or future, of significant quantities of Soviet arms to North Vietnam by sea."[6] On occasion Soviet officials threatened to ship goods by sea, and First Secretary Yuri Loginov in London "painted [a] dark picture of inevitable US-Soviet naval confrontation should USG resort to blockade and mining."[7] But a report from March 1967 confirmed that during February 1967 "No imports of arms or ammunition by sea were detected."[8]

Arguably, Moscow's "special area of responsibility" for providing North Vietnam with a viable air defense was its Achilles Heel, which the United States sought to exploit.[9] A May 1967 report by Walt Rostow discussed the adverse effects of the war on Moscow, in particular "the bombing of North Vietnam constitutes a continuing reproach to the Soviet Union, unable as it is to protect a small ally." Due to Vietnam's geographical location "Moscow cannot feasibly undertake any serious military participation in the war, with its own combat forces, far from the sources of Soviet power, and at the end of lines of communication passing through the dubiously friendly territory of China or risking US counteraction at sea." But they were unable to "force a blockade or to confront the US with a major military challenge," which really

5 CIA, Special National Intelligence Estimate Number 10-6-65, "Probable Communist Reactions to Certain US Actions," Top Secret/Declassified 9/8/1994, 2 June 1965, NSF National Intelligence Estimates, Box 1, Folder 8, Document 7a, LBJPL.

6 CIA Memorandum, "Soviet Maritime Activity and North Vietnam," Top Secret Dinar/Declassified with Redactions 8/11/1998, 2 April 1965, Box 49, Folder 5, Document 11, National Security File, Country File, Vietnam, LBJPL.

7 State Department, London Embassy to SecState, "Soviet Policy on Viet Nam," Confidential/Declassified 2/27/2007, 31 May 1967, NSF Country File Vietnam, Box 44, Folder 1, Document 35b, LBJPL.

8 CIA Memorandum entitled "Foreign Shipping to North Vietnam in February 1967," Secret/Declassified and Sanitized on 4/27/1993, 22 March 1967, NSF Country File-Vietnam, Box 42, Folder 3, Document 93, LBJ Library.

9 CIA, National Intelligence Estimate Number 11-16-66, "Current Soviet Attitudes Toward the US," Secret/Sanitized 6/23/2008, 28 July 1966, NSF National Intelligence Estimates, Box 3, Folder 6, Document 23, LBJPL.

meant that they "have no alternative but to help Hanoi to carry on the war."[10] In effect, Moscow was trapped.

The U.S. Navy had unchallenged sea control off the coast of North Vietnam. Coincidentally, on 9 March 1965, a Soviet ambassador acknowledged the United States had bombed one SAM base in Vietnam, plus sank "a ship carrying missiles."[11] This admission seemed to confirm that the U.S. Navy was actually blockading Soviet munitions ships. Frustrated by having to use only land routes through China, during March 1965 one Soviet official even admitted that the U.S. policy "is coming dangerously close to 'boxing in' the governing authorities in the USSR."[12] Because of the intentional sinking of a Soviet cargo ship carrying missiles, "the Chinese action [limiting shipments] must have demonstrated to Hanoi the degree of its dependence on Peking in obtaining all block military assistance."[13] The U.S. government sought to further exploit these tensions to turn the USSR and China from unhappy cobelligerents into active enemies.

---

10 Walt Rostow to the President, Memorandum, Secret/Declassified 8/14/1995, 5 May 1967, NSF Country File Vietnam, Box 43, Folder 1, Document 47, LBJPL.

11 CIA Memorandum, "Alleged Imminent Stationing of Soviet Missiles," Secret/ Sanitized, 15 March 1965, Box 15, Folder 2, Document 118, National Security File, Country File, Vietnam, LBJPL.

12 CIA Memorandum, "The Situation in Vietnam," Top Secret/Sanitized, 20 March 1965, Box 49, Folder 5, Document 17, National Security File, Country File, Vietnam, LBJPL.

13 CIA Intelligence Memorandum entitled "The Chinese Position in North Vietnam," Secret/Declassified on 12/16/1993, 8 August 1966, NSF Country File-Vietnam, Box 35, Folder 3, Document 153, LBJPL.

Chapter 18

THE SECRET U.S. ANTI-SAM STRATEGY IN THE VIETNAM WAR (1966)

The main U.S. Cold War strategy was to turn China against the USSR. Every Russian-made SAM transferred to North Vietnam through China added incrementally to the seriousness of the Sino-Soviet rift. In 1965, the USSR sent North Vietnam 80 million dollars-worth of SAMs and launchers, or about 60% of the $142,000,000 million in Soviet military aid.[1] On 16 February 1966, it was reported that North Vietnam had a total of 84 SAM sites, which was an increase of 21 sites during recent weeks. But this report concluded: "In terms of actual threat, the expansion of prepared firing positions does not increase DRV capabilities to deter US air operations."[2] A later estimate put it closer to 130 SAM sites. Coincidentally, American bomber runs sought to soak up the maximum number of SAMs, since having to import new ones through China dramatically increased Sino-Soviet tensions.

The surface-to-air missiles provided by the USSR posed a huge threat to American planes. But as of 17 August 1966, only 26 planes had been shot down by SAMs, as compared to 272 brought down by AA fire: "Surface-to-Air missile defenses have played a significant role in inflicting losses, not by direct effects, but by forcing attack aircraft down into the range of anti-aircraft guns." Still, the 384 lost aircraft out of 100,784 sorties equalled only 0.3%, "which has been somewhat less than predicted."[3] A secret American goal was to increase dramatically the number of SAMs the USSR shipped to North Vietnam through China. While only 200 SAMs were provided in 1965, and 1,100 in 1966, in just the first six months of 1967 alone an estimated 1,750

---

1 CIA statistics, Top Secret Trine, 1 June 1966, NSF Country File Vietnam, Box 51, Folder 4, Document 49b, LBJPL.

2 CIA, "Intelligence Memorandum, DRV SAM Defense Expanding," Top Secret, 16 February 1966, NSF Country File Vietnam, Box 51, Folder 2, Document 25, LBJPL.

3 Memorandum by Arthur McCaffety for the President entitled "U.S. Bombing Missions over North Vietnam," Secret/Declassified on 3/18/1994, 17 August 1966, NSF Country File-Vietnam, Box 35, Folder 2, Document 108, LBJPL.

SAMs were sent to North Vietnam, valued at $52 million, one of the single largest components of the $220 million in Soviet aid.[4] A major U.S. goal was to put additional pressure on this supply line. As Walt Rostow told LBJ on 11 February 1967, "the trouble in China may affect supplies to Hanoi," which makes it "clear the Chinese are trying to force a break in relations with Moscow"[5] (see Map 8).

Of course, U.S. airmen were not told that the real goal behind bombing North Vietnam was to soak up as many SAMs as possible. Chief of Naval Operations David McDonald reported in September 1966 that aircrews criticized guidelines requiring repetitive air attacks that seemed more than anything else to benefit enemy gunners. When Senator Symington visited South Vietnam during late 1966, he made a point of emphasizing to Westmoreland that "Restrictions relative to attack on targets in North Vietnam impact unfavorably on US pilot morale," and he opposed "repetitive pilot tours."[6] But these critiques actually confirm that the true goal of the bombing runs was to soak up the maximum number of SAMs as possible.

During 1967, in the second full year of *Rolling Thunder* some 362 U.S. aircraft were lost over North Vietnam. During late November 1967, the White House situation room reported that because the bombing was focused on Hanoi, which had the best air defenses, "new records were set in the number of US aircraft downed (18), in the number of surface-to-air missiles fired in one week (299) and in the number of US aircraft downed by missiles in one week (10)."[7] Many pilots were rescued, but many others became POWs. For example, John McCain's A4 was shot down by a SAM while attacking the Hanoi Thermal Power Plant on 26 October 1967, and he subsequently spent years as a POW.

But Operation *Rolling Thunder* was specifically intended to exert pressure on Russia and China. After 14,557 sorties only 108 aircraft had been shot down. On 2 June 1966, this operation's impact was boiled down and it was

---

4 CIA, "Intelligence Memorandum: Assessment of a Postulated Agreement on US and Soviet Actions in North Vietnam," Top Secret Trine, 4 August 1967, NSF Country File Vietnam, Box 51, Folder 5, Document 27, LBJPL.

5 Letter from W.W.R. to the President, Top Secret, 11 February 1967, NSF Country File Vietnam, Box 51, Folder 3, Document 10, LBJPL.

6 Memorandum "To the President from General Westmoreland in Saigon," Secret/Declassified 1/30/1984, 3 January 1967, Box 39, Folder 3, Document 115a, National Security File, Country File, Vietnam, LBJPL.

7 White House Situation Room to the President, "Situation Room Report for the President," Top Secret/Declassified 6/3/1993, 25 November 1967, NSF Country File Vietnam, Box 104, Folder 2, Document 76, LBJPL.

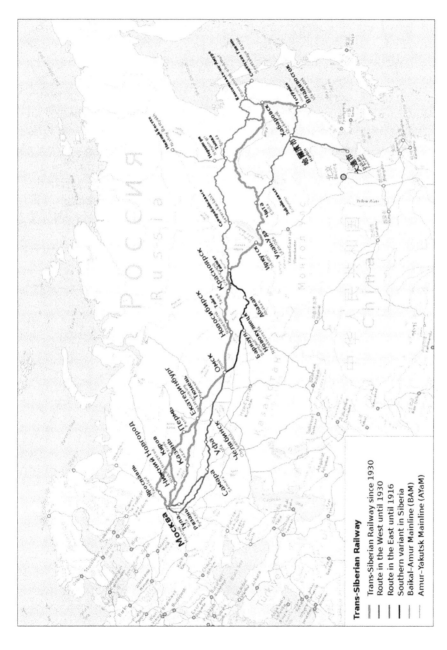

Map 8 Missile transportation from USSR through China to North Vietnam.

determined that the bombing had dramatically increased tensions between the Chinese and Soviets. This positive outcome was only included in the original version of an Alternatives paper written by Bill Jorden in early June 1966. As Rostow told the president on 2 June 1966, it was removed from the sanitized version of the Alternatives paper. Why was it removed? Clearly, because it was considered to be the single most important—albeit secret—part of the report.

Edwin Reischauer in early 1967 warned Washington that air strikes against North Vietnam represented "a complete psychological blunder" in believing that "the bombing can punish the enemy enough to make him want to negotiate."[8] But the documents cited here show that this was never the only reason for the bombing. The most important reason was to put supreme pressure on the Sino-Soviet alliance by maximizing SAM deliveries from the USSR, through China. This strategy succeeded beyond all expectations. The two countries soon went to war along their mutual border on 2 March 1969.

---

8 Memorandum entitled "Edwin Reischauer on Vietnam," 1–2 February 1967, Box 40, Folder 5, Document 131, National Security File, Country File, Vietnam, LBJPL.

Chapter 19

THE 3 MARCH 1969 CREATION OF THE TOP GUN SCHOOL (1969)

Once it became clear that Sino-Soviet tensions had reached new heights, on 31 October 1968 President Johnson ordered that all air, naval and artillery bombardment of North Vietnam would end as of 1 November 1968. His stated goal was to open talks leading to a negotiated peace settlement, but arguably Johnson's real goal was to turn China and the USSR against each other even more. This plan worked. On 2 March 1969, conflict erupted along China's northern border with Russia. For a time, it even appeared this war might spread and perhaps even go nuclear. Although this did not happen, the Sino-Soviet war opened the door for the next American president, Richard M. Nixon, to begin the long process of opening diplomatic relations with China and turning the PRC against the USSR. Coincidentally, the U.S. Navy's Top Gun School also opened on 3 March 1969, just one day after the Sino-Soviet war erupted, since the previous goal of soaking up SAMs was no longer required.

In December 1966, the CIA reported Hanoi thought "the Vietnam war was a test case as to whether world communism would succeed or not."[1] President Johnson's strategy of tearing apart the Sino-Soviet alliance by focusing on Soviet aid to North Vietnam worked perfectly, since all such aid had to transit through Chinese territory. Soaking up the maximum number of SAMs was critical for this plan to succeed. By February 1967, the CIA could report: "The internal turmoil in China with its anti-Soviet theme has greatly reduced the amount of Soviet aid reaching North Vietnam. The Soviets have

---

1 CIA Intelligence Information Cable, "Comments on the Vietnam Situation and Relations with Various Foreign Countries," Secret/Declassified and Sanitized 6/11/1998, 19 December 1966, Box 40, Folder 158, Document 105a, National Security File, Country File, Vietnam, LBJPL.

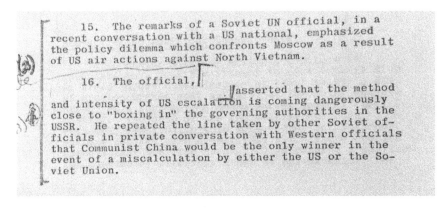

15. The remarks of a Soviet UN official, in a recent conversation with a US national, emphasized the policy dilemma which confronts Moscow as a result of US air actions against North Vietnam.

16. The official, ⟦   ⟧asserted that the method and intensity of US escalation is coming dangerously close to "boxing in" the governing authorities in the USSR. He repeated the line taken by other Soviet officials in private conversation with Western officials that Communist China would be the only winner in the event of a miscalculation by either the US or the Soviet Union.

Document 8 Soviet official warns China would be only winner.

tried to bypass the problem by transporting the material by air but lack sufficient long-range planes to accomplish the task."[2]

As early as spring 1965, it became clear to the CIA that the way to play the USSR and China off each other was the delivery of military aid to North Vietnam. The U.S. bombing campaign sought to increase Soviet-Soviet tensions. The USSR soon began to feel trapped. Frustrated, during March 1965 one Soviet official even warned "that Communist China would be the only winner in the event of a miscalculation by either the US or the Soviet Union"[3] (see Document 8).

Against Moscow's wishes, "the Chinese action [limiting shipments] must have demonstrated to Hanoi the degree of its dependence on Peking in obtaining all block military assistance."[4] But such shipping delays, especially of SAMs, negatively impacted Sino-Soviet relations. As early as 23 March 1967, the CIA reported that the New Delhi "Indian Express" was saying that the "Soviet Union was considering the possibility of routing the air transport of military materiel destined for North Vietnam via India, Burma and

2 CIA Intelligence Information Cable, "State of Morale in North Vietnam and Sincerity of Willingness to Negotiate Peace," Secret/Declassified and Sanitized 4/15/1993, 7 February 1967, Box 40, Folder 4, Document 105a, National Security File, Country File, Vietnam, LBJPL.

3 CIA Memorandum, "The Situation in Vietnam," Top Secret/Sanitized, 20 March 1965, Box 49, Folder 5, Document 17, National Security File, Country File, Vietnam, LBJPL.

4 CIA Intelligence Memorandum entitled "The Chinese Position in North Vietnam," Secret/Declassified on 12/16/1993, 8 August 1966, NSF Country File-Vietnam, Box 35, Folder 3, Document 153, LBJPL.

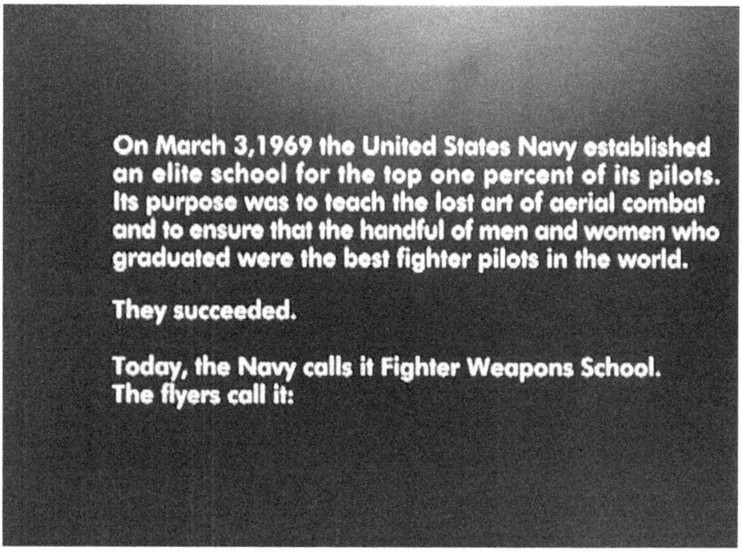

On March 3,1969 the United States Navy established an elite school for the top one percent of its pilots. Its purpose was to teach the lost art of aerial combat and to ensure that the handful of men and women who graduated were the best fighter pilots in the world.

They succeeded.

Today, the Navy calls it Fighter Weapons School. The flyers call it:

Picture 8 Top Gun School opens one day after Sino-Soviet war begins.

Laos, to avoid complications such as were recently created by the Chinese Communists."[5] Thereafter, in July 1968, Beijing for the first time absolutely refused to allow three trains of materiel destined for Vietnam to transit Chinese territory.

This Chinese action proved that President Johnson's peripheral campaign in Vietnam had been a complete success. By now the Sino-Soviet break seemed complete. On 2 March 1969, just as Johnson had hoped, the USSR and the PRC went to war along China's northern border. This war was a direct result of the U.S. policies in Vietnam. Coincidentally, now that soaking up the maximum number of SAMs was no longer necessary, on 3 March 1969 the Top Gun School opened. One of the school's goals was to train U.S. pilots in how to better avoid being hit by SAMs. This development was mentioned prominently in the recent Hollywood film *Top Gun: Maverick* (see Picture 8).

---

5 CIA Intelligence Information Cable entitled "Comments of North Vietnamese Diplomat," Secret/Declassified and Sanitized on 4/27/1993, 23 March 1967, NSF Country File-Vietnam, Box 35, Folder 3, Document 153, LBJPL.

Chapter 20

THE REAL "SIGNALING" HISTORY OF THE 4 MAY 1970 KENT STATE MASSACRE (1970)

After the Sino-Soviet war broke out on 2 March 1969, both Washington and Beijing engaged in a diplomatic "dance" to signal that they sought to open diplomatic relations. The 4 May 1970 dating of the Kent State Massacre that killed four students is highly coincidental, therefore, in particular considering the historical importance of the 4 May 1919 student protests against the Paris Peace Treaty (see Picture 9). As mentioned earlier, news of the transfer of the Shandong concession to Japan was initially released on 30 April 1919, but Japan's statement of intent was not widely published. In China, public demonstrations and student protests indicated that Chinese dissatisfaction was widespread, as student groups marched through the foreign legation quarter on 4 May 1919, and left protests at the American, British, French and Italian embassies. When the police arrested 32 students, one was killed, which caused further demonstrations. These events later resulted in the creation of the Chinese Communist Party in July 1921.

As mentioned earlier, Wilson's secretary mistakenly never published the compromise Wilson had negotiated with Japan. This coincidental oversight proved to be fatal. By 20 May 1919, the "May Fourth Movement" had expanded and students from middle schools and universities in Peking went on strike. The center of the movement then shifted to Shanghai, where a general strike of students, workers, and businessmen swelled to 100,000 and paralyzed Shanghai.[1] Terms for the return of Shandong were agreed to at the Washington Conference in 1921–22. But, as long as China refused to sign the Versailles Peace Treaty, Japan could not carry out arrangements to transfer the Shandong concessions to China. Furthermore, during this more than two-year delay the Chinese Communist Party was founded during July 1921,

---

1 Wang Shih-han, "May 4th Movement," *China Reconstructs* (Peking, 1962), 64.

Picture 9 Demonstrations at Kent State on 4 May 1970 resulting in four deaths.

in part due to the Shandong controversy. Therefore, the 51st anniversary of the 4 May 1919 movement held great meaning for Chinese revolutionaries.

Sino-Soviet tensions resulting from the 2 March 1969 border war presented President Richard Nixon a rare opportunity to combine forces with China to exert greater pressure on the USSR and, over the long term, induce its economic collapse. On 4 August 1969, President Nixon called Moscow the main aggressor in the Sino-Soviet border conflict and argued that a Chinese defeat would be contrary to U.S. interests. This comment indicated a shift from the U.S. policy of isolating China, which led to a lengthy "dance" as Washington and Beijing opened secret talks. But when Nixon authorized the April 1970 invasion of Cambodia, a student demonstration at Kent State broke out on exactly 4 May 1970. It seems hard to believe that the choice of dates was purely coincidental. It might have been a Chinese "signal." The National Guard shot and killed four students; interestingly, the number four in Mandarin Chinese signifies "death."

The American public was outraged and demanded the United States end the war in Vietnam. In the immediate aftermath of the Kent State Massacre, there was an intensification beginning in September 1970 of secret White House attempts to open talks with China. In July 1971, U.S. secretary of state Henry Kissinger made a secret trip to Beijing in preparation for President

Nixon's trip the next year. Nixon had two objectives: extrication from the Vietnam War and victory in the Cold War against the USSR.

In what must have seemed to many Chinese as an American tributary mission to China, President Nixon flew to China in 1972 to meet with Mao Zedong. They signed the *Shanghai Communiqué*, the first of three communiqués issued in 1972, 1979 and 1982, respectively. The *Shanghai Communiqué* provided two interpretations of the status of Taiwan. While China again declared Taiwan to be its province, the U.S. agreed not to challenge the view shared by "all Chinese" on both sides of the Taiwan Strait that "there is but one China and that Taiwan is part of China."[2]

While formal diplomatic relations would not be reestablished until 1979, the subject of the second communiqué, the long period of Sino-American estrangement had ended. On 25 October 1971, Taiwan lost its seat at the United Nations. Henceforth, the PRC sat on the Security Council as one of the five privileged nations to possess veto power, along with the USSR, the United States, France and Great Britain, the victorious powers at the end of World War II when the United Nations was established. These watershed events might not have happened without the Kent State Massacre, which is why the 4 May 1970 date of these demonstrations—the 51st anniversary of the May Fourth Movement in China—appears to be not quite so coincidental after all. This event may have been a signal to Washington secretly orchestrated by Beijing.

---

2 "Joint Communiqué," 28 February 1972, http://edition.cnn.com/SPECIALS/cold. war/episodes/15/documents/us.china/.

Chapter 21

THE SECRET AGREEMENT THAT MAY HAVE REALLY ENDED THE VIETNAM WAR (1975)

As North Vietnam was invading South Vietnam during spring 1975, the U.S. ambassador in Saigon, Graham Martin, reported that North Vietnam was claiming they had a secret agreement with Washington, saying of North Vietnamese officials, "they would love to have you sit down with Le Duc Tho in order to confirm the rumors they are spreading through South Vietnam that this offensive is part of a deal they we have made with them" (see Document 9). Coincidentally, during May 1972, Kissinger did appear to have made just such a secret deal with Brezhnev. In return for the USSR cutting its arms exports to North Vietnam, the United States agreed to allow North Vietnam to invade the South a year-and-a-half after the peace treaty was signed and went into force.

If the goal of the Vietnam War was to divide the USSR and China, that goal absolutely succeeded on 2 March 1969. When holding U.S.-Soviet discussions in Moscow on how best to end the war in Vietnam, a deal appears to have been struck. During secret talks between Nixon, Brezhnev and Kosygin in May 1972, Kosygin reassured Nixon "there is not a single ship on the way to Vietnam now carrying military equipment—not one shell—only flour and foodstuffs, no armaments whatever" (see Document 10). Cutting North Vietnam off from Soviet weapons was clearly intended to put pressure on Hanoi to come to terms with Washington.

In return, the U.S. government made its own offer. If the USSR would help convince Hanoi to sign a peace agreement, preferably before Nixon's second term in office began, then after a certain amount of time—in this case 18 months—the U.S. government "would be agreeable to the Vietnamese doing whatever they want" (see Document 11).

Without Soviet backing, Hanoi had little choice but to open peace talks with the United States. A peace agreement ending the Vietnam War was in fact signed in Paris on 27 January 1973, just a week after Nixon was

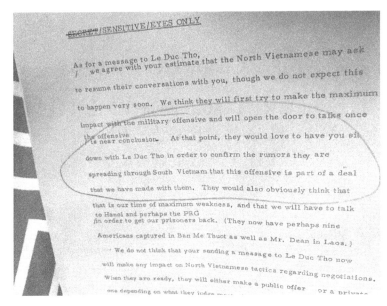

As for a message to Le Duc Tho, we agree with your estimate that the North Vietnamese may ask to resume their conversations with you, though we do not expect this to happen very soon. We think they will first try to make the maximum impact with the military offensive and will open the door to talks once the offensive is near conclusion. At that point, they would love to have you sit down with Le Duc Tho in order to confirm the rumors they are spreading through South Vietnam that this offensive is part of a deal that we have made with them. They would also obviously think that that is our time of maximum weakness, and that we will have to talk to Hanoi and perhaps the PRG in order to get our prisoners back. (They now have perhaps nine Americans captured in Ban Me Thuot as well as Mr. Dean in Laos.)

We do not think that your sending a message to Le Duc Tho now will make any impact on North Vietnamese tactics regarding negotiations. When they are ready, they will either make a public offer or a private one depending on what they judge ...

Document 9   North Vietnamese officials claim there is a secret deal.

TOP SECRET/SENSITIVE/
EXCLUSIVELY EYES ONLY

General Secretary Brezhnev: It has been in the TASS communication.

Chairman Kosygin: I refer once again to the Minister of Marines' report on our ships being buzzed and bombs being dropped near them and American aircraft imitating bombing dives against our ships.

The President: We will check. That's against our orders.

General Secretary Brezhnev: You can appreciate our feeling on this matter, because when one of our ships was damaged and some people were wounded before your visit we lodged a protest with you, but we didn't say one word about this in the Soviet press. The entire world knew about it.

Chairman Kosygin: Another thing, there is not a single ship on the way to Vietnam now carrying military equipment -- not one shell -- only flour and foodstuffs, no armaments whatever.

... went upstairs to dinner.

Document 10   Kosygin reassures Nixon no weapons being shipped.

... or non-communist, that is their business.

Dr. Kissinger told me that if there was a peaceful settlement in Vietnam you would be agreeable to the Vietnamese doing whatever they want, having whatever they want after a period of time, say 18 months. If that is indeed true, and if the Vietnamese knew this, and it was true, they would be sympathetic on that basis. Even from the point of view of the election in the United States I submit that the end of the war at this particular time would play a positive role whereas escalation will not. As for sending in new waves of bombers against Vietnam, they cannot solve the problem and never can.

Document 11   Secret U.S.-Soviet deal to end the Vietnam War.

States, I have wondered a good deal about whether or not we're

following the right course of action in killing as many North

Vietnamese as we're killing, because if Red China is a real

threat in the future then the most war-like people in South-

east Asia are the Vietnamese and I would be perfectly delighted

to see a lot of North Vietnamese in the way if Red China de-

cided it was going to start to march.

Document 12 Clark Clifford's 13 March 1969 talk.

inaugurated for his second term. By this point Brezhnev had certainly passed on Nixon's offer. Almost exactly a year-and-a-half after the peace agreement went into effect during summer 1973, North Vietnam did successfully invade South Vietnam during spring 1975, and the United States did not intervene to oppose it. North Vietnamese officials even bragged about this secret agreement.

The rapid collapse of South Vietnam appeared to take Washington by surprise. The chaotic nature of the American withdrawal from Saigon is proof of that. But this chaos was perhaps intended to cover up that a secret deal already existed. Ambassador Graham Martin constantly complained about the lack of proper evacuation planning, but perhaps Washington wanted the withdrawal to look convincing to Beijing. Meanwhile, it was much better for Washington in the long run to have a united and strong Vietnam on China's southern border. This was largely in line with Clark Clifford's 13 March 1969 talk discussing how best to contain China (see Document 12).

Washington's hopes that a united Vietnam would halt Chinese expansion southward were soon rewarded. In September 1975, Le Duan, the secretary-general of the Communist Party of Vietnam, traveled to China. Beijing warned Le Duan that it was concerned about Vietnam's close relations with the USSR, and tried to push Hanoi into siding with China: "The breakdown of Vietnam's relations with China after 1975 and Vietnam's current pro-Soviet alignment may be traced to Vietnamese resistance to Chinese pressures to take sides."[1] When Hanoi resisted, Beijing threatened it with severe consequences. Part of China's "punishment" for Vietnam's lack of support occurred in 1976, when "China recalled several groups of specialists from

---

1 Ramesh Thaku and Carlyle Thayer, *Soviet Relations with India and Vietnam* (New York: St. Martin's Press, 1992), 287.

Vietnam and delayed work on a number of projects being built with Chinese aid."[2]

Meanwhile, by the summer of 1978, Sino-Soviet tensions also intensified, as reflected by increased Soviet troop concentrations along the Sino-Soviet border. During September 1978, the USSR increased arms shipments to Vietnam, both by air and by sea. These included "aircraft, missiles, tanks, and munitions."[3] This culminated on 2 November 1978, when the two countries signed a Treaty of Friendship and Cooperation. This treaty was clearly aimed at China, since one clause stated that Vietnam and the USSR would "immediately consult each other" if either is "attacked or threatened with attack [...] with a view to eliminating that threat."[4] Reportedly, a secret protocol also granted Soviet military forces access to Vietnam's "airfields and ports."[5]

Meanwhile, Vietnam prepared to invade Cambodia.[6] Beijing, in turn, tried to outflank Moscow. On 15 December 1978, China announced that Sino-American relations would be normalized in Washington on 1 January 1979. Soon after this announcement, Vietnam attacked Cambodia, and by 7 January 1979, Vietnamese forces had secured Phnom Penh. The timing of these events was critical, and the USSR's and China's new alliances were closely linked: "Thus two strategic alliances had been created in the closing months of 1978, a Soviet-Vietnamese alliance and a Sino-American alliance, and they would prevail for about a decade."[7]

China's 1979 invasion into Vietnam was also linked to Hanoi's new treaty with Moscow. Deng Xiaoping stated that the 1978 Soviet-Vietnamese "military alliance" was really just part of the USSR's long-time goal to "encircle China." In the wake of Vietnam's successful occupation of Cambodia, it was "the resultant Soviet encirclement of China [that] necessitated a limited invasion of Vietnam."[8] According to King C. Chen: "Had there been no Soviet-Vietnamese alliance, the sixteen-day war between China and Vietnam might

2 Stephen J. Morris, *Why Vietnam Invaded Cambodia: Political Culture and the Causes of War* (Stanford: Stanford University Press, 1999), 174.

3 Robert S. Ross, *The Indochina Tangle* (New York: Columbia University Press, 1988), 208.

4 *FBIS SU,* 6 November 1978, 6–9.

5 Thaku and Thayer, *Soviet Relations with India and Vietnam*, 61.

6 William J. Duiker, *China and Vietnam: The Roots of Conflict* (Berkeley, CA: Institute of East Asian Studies, 1986), 80.

7 Ramses Amer, "Sino-Vietnamese normalization in the light of the crisis of the late 1970s," *Pacific Affairs*, Volume 67, No. 3 (fall 1994), 362–363.

8 Ross, *The Indochina Tangle*, 217, 225.

help neither you nor us."
Raúl interrupted. "We are very aware of this. ...We understand it very well.
It is as obvious as two plus two equals four." Cuba was not asking the Soviets to
promise to intervene militarily on its behalf. Nor was it asking that the Soviet
Union resort to nuclear weapons to defend Cuba. "For our Political Bureau, for
Comrade Fidel and even for the most immature Cuban communist it would be
immoral to ask the Soviet Union to start a nuclear war on our behalf. This idea
doesn't cross anybody's mind." What Cuba wanted, he repeated, was a Soviet
warning to the United States. But Andropov poured cold water on the idea. "We
can't agree to any declaration that would threaten the United States. Because
what leverage could we bring to bear? Before the Chinese attacked Vietnam
[in February 1979], we made the kind of declaration you're talking about, don't
touch Vietnam, because otherwise ... The Chinese laughed at us and got on
with their business. If we're going to make threats we have to have some means
to back them up."

Andropov did not question the gravity of the U.S. threat against Cuba. He

Document 13 China ignores Soviet threats not to attack Vietnam. Source: Piero
Gleijeses, *Visions of Freedom: Havana, Washington, Pretoria, and the Struggle
for Southern Africa, 1976–1991* (Chapel Hill: The University of North
Carolina Press, 2013), 217.

not have been fought."[9] When Moscow warned Beijing that it might intervene, China ignored them (see Document 13).

Although these Asian events during the 1970s may have looked confusing
to outsiders, in return for allowing the United States to withdraw from the
Vietnam War with honor, North Vietnam was secretly allowed to reunify
with the South. Unified Vietnam then put pressure on China, which in turn
pushed Beijing into turning to Washington for support: official Sino-U.S.
diplomatic relations were opened on 1 January 1979. Thereafter, turning
the combined forces of NATO in the West and China on the East against
the USSR set up a pincer movement that—10 years later—resulted in the
fall of the Berlin Wall, the end of the Cold War, and two years after that,
the collapse of the USSR. In essence, Johnson's secret strategy to use the
Vietnam War to break apart the Sino-Soviet alliance, when combined with
the 1972 Nixon-Brezhnev secret agreement ending the Vietnam War, eventually won the Cold War.

Coincidentally, these two diplomatic victories may have been the one-two
punch that ultimately destroyed the USSR.

---

9 King C. Chen, *China's War with Vietnam, 1979* (Stanford, CA: Hoover Institution Press,
1987), 27.

CONCLUSIONS: THE PROFOUND INFLUENCE OF COINCIDENTAL HISTORY ON TWENTIETH-CENTURY HISTORY

This short book has attempted to reveal a number of what might first appear to be random historical coincidences. These coincidences profoundly impacted U.S. and British history. For example, in 1897 the president of the U.S. Naval War College talked to Theodore Roosevelt about the importance of securing naval bases in the Pacific, and the very next year it coincidentally happened. Or how the Entente's invasion of Gallipoli just happened to overlap exactly with the Armenian genocide. Or how the date 7 December appeared not just once, but three times in 1902, 1917 and 1941. To cite James Bond-creator Ian Fleming's famous quote: "Once is happenstance. Twice is coincidence. Three times is enemy action."

Many coincidences also impacted communist countries, in particular the Soviet Union. For example, gold was coincidentally discovered in Outer Mongolia immediately before it became a Soviet protectorate. The Great Purges and the expansion of Siberian gulags took place right after Japan coincidentally announced a major 5-million-person immigration push into Manchukuo. And Stalin was coincidentally able to make use of what appeared to be random word changes in the Yalta agreement and in Truman's Order No. 1 to obtain huge swaths of Asian territory, including the southern Kuriles, Outer Mongolia and many points along the still-disputed Sino-Russian border.

China was equally impacted by coincidence. General Yuan Shikai appears to have preapproved Japan's 21 Demands against China in return for being made monarch. Severe student unrest due to the perceived unfairness of the Paris Peace Treaty in 1919 might have been easily assuaged if only Wilson's secretary had published his compromise agreement with Japan, which the secretary coincidentally refused to do. In 1970, China might have then coincidentally used the anniversary of the May Fourth Movement to send a potent signal to Washington promoting the opening of diplomatic relations. Finally, and arguably most importantly, in 1948 the CIA suggested that to maximize Sino-Soviet tensions the Chinese communists should be allowed to take all of Mainland China, and in fact just 10 years later the Sino-Soviet alliance split, and 10 years after that—following the intentional intensification of Sino-Soviet tensions due to the Vietnam War—the two countries went to war, thereby opening the door for a Sino-U.S. rapprochement.

The Vietnam War was also clearly impacted by coincidence. In variance with accepted wisdom, the second Tonkin Gulf attack on 4 August 1964 might have actually taken place. The U.S. Navy might have been carrying out an active blockade of North Vietnam, including possibly sinking one or more Soviet cargo ships carrying missiles to Hanoi. The highly secret anti-SAM strategy might have coincidentally resulted in the 2 March 1969 Sino-Soviet border conflict, just as the creation of the Top Gun School, coincidentally on the very next day, 3 March 1969, helped make these SAMs less effective at shooting down American planes. And, last but not least, the secret agreement negotiated by President Nixon ending the Vietnam War might have coincidentally resulted in the winning of the Cold War.

Can these coincidences be proven? No, they cannot. Definitive documentation simply does not exist at this time to prove these events are linked one way or the other. Hopefully future historians will be on the lookout for additional documents that could substantiate these incidents. Some of these historical coincidences were absolutely critical, however, like the possible genocide of perhaps a million Christian Armenians so they would not be able to assist the Gallipoli invaders, while other coincidences pertained to disputed boundaries and captured islands, like those in the southern Kuriles and along the Sino-Russian border, still unresolved to this day. Perhaps some of these border disputes could even be finally solved over time, in particular if greater knowledge of the facts were to come out.

But what is most important to keep in mind in our age of instant information—the internet, Wikipedia and social media—is that it should never be overlooked that we don't know everything. Far from it. Many secrets remain. Many archives, libraries and private papers are as yet untapped. Many mysteries are still out there for the intrepid researcher just waiting to be solved. Contrary to popular belief, history is not over. Future international historians should never assume, therefore, that everything is already known under the sun. Or, as a 7 July 2023 *WSJ* article perhaps put it best, American diplomats posted to Russia receive special guidelines informally known as "Moscow Rules." One important rule, said the officials who helped to craft it: "There are no coincidences."

BIBLIOGRAPHY

Beloff, Max, *Soviet Far Eastern Policy Since Yalta* (New York: Institute of Pacific Relations, 1950).

Campi, Alicia J., "The Political Relationship Between the United States and Outer Mongolia, 1915–1927: The Kalgan Consular Records," Indiana University Dissertation, 1988.

Chang, Gordan H., *Friends and Enemies: The United States, China, and the Soviet Union, 1948–1972* (Stanford: Stanford University Press, 1990).

Chen, King C., *China's War with Vietnam, 1979* (Stanford, CA: Hoover Institution Press, 1987).

Chiang Kai-shek, *China's Destiny* (New York: The MacMillan Company, 1947).

Day, Alan J., ed., *Border and Territorial Disputes*, Keesings Reference Publication (Detroit: Gale Research Co., 1982).

Doolin, Dennis J., *Territorial Claims in the Sino-Soviet Conflict* (Stanford, CA: Hoover Institution Studies: 7, 1965).

Duiker, William J., *China and Vietnam: The Roots of Conflict* (Berkeley, CA: Institute of East Asian Studies, 1986).

Elleman, Bruce A., *Diplomacy and Deception: The Secret History of Sino-Soviet Diplomatic Relations, 1917–1927* (Armonk, NY: M.E. Sharpe, 1997).

———, *Wilson and China: A Revised History of the Shandong Question* (Armonk, NY: M.E. Sharpe, 2002).

———, *Japanese-American Civilian Prisoner Exchanges and Detention Camps, 19421–45* (New York: Routledge Press, 2006).

———, *International Rivalry and Secret Diplomacy in East Asia, 1896–1950* (London: Routledge, 2019).

———, *The United States Navy's Pivot to Asia: The Origins of "A Cooperative Strategy for Twenty-First Century Seapower"* (London: Routledge Press, 2023).

———, *Taiwan's Offshore Islands: Pathway or Barrier?* (Newport, RI: NWC Press, 2019).

———, *The Making of the Modern Chinese Navy: Special Historical Characteristics* (London: Anthem Press, 2019).

———, *International Rivalry and Secret Diplomacy in East Asia, 1896–1950* (London: Routledge, 2019).

———, *A History of the Modern Chinese Navy: 1840–2020* (New York: Routledge, 2021).

———, *Taiwan Straits Standoff: 70 Years of PRC-Taiwan Cross-Strait Tensions* (London: Anthem Press, 2022).

———, *Principles of Maritime Power* (Lanham, MD: Rowman & Littlefield, 2022).

———, and S.C.M. Paine, eds., *Naval Power and Expeditionary Warfare: Peripheral Campaigns and New Theatres of Naval Warfare* (New York: Routledge, 2012).

————, and S.C.M. Paine, eds., *Commerce Raiding: Historical Case Studies, 1755–2009* (Newport, RI: NWC Press, 2013).

————, and S.C.M. Paine, eds., *Navies and Soft Power: Historical Case Studies of Naval Power and the Nonuse of Military Force* (Newport, RI: NWC Press, 2015).

Hayes, Rosemary, *The Northern Territorial Issue* (Arlington, VA: Institute for Defense Analyses, 1972).

Hsü, Immanuel C. Y., *The Rise of Modern China* (New York: Oxford Press, 1990).

Jones, Jerry W., *U.S. Battleship Operations in World War I* (Annapolis: Naval Institute Press, 1998).

Khrushchev, Nikita Sergeevich, and Sergei Khrushchev, *Memoirs of Nikita Khrushchev: Statesman, 1953–1964* (College Park: Penn State Press, 2007).

Lu Ch'iu-wen, *Chung-e Wai-meng Chiao-she Shih-mo* (The Ins and Outs of Sino-Russian Negotiations on Outer Mongolia) (Taipei: Cheng-wen Publishing Company, 1976).

Miller, Edward S., *War Plan Orange: The U.S. Strategy to Defeat Japan 1897–1945* (Annapolis, MD: Naval Institute Press, 2007).

Morris, Stephen J., *Why Vietnam Invaded Cambodia: Political Culture and the Causes of War* (Stanford: Stanford University Press, 1999).

Rees, David, *The Soviet Seizure of the Kuriles* (New York: Praeger Publishers, 1985).

Ross, Robert S., *The Indochina Tangle* (New York: Columbia University Press, 1988).

Rupen, Robert, *How Mongolia Is Really Ruled: A Political History of the Mongolian People's Republic 1900–1978* (Stanford, CA: Stanford University Press, 1979).

Sims, Rear Admiral William Sowden, *The Victory at Sea* (New York: Doubleday, 1920; reprinted Annapolis: Naval Institute Press, 1984).

Snell, John L., ed., *The Meaning of Yalta* (Baton Rouge: Louisiana State University Press, 1956).

Stephan, John J., *The Kuril Islands: Russo-Japanese Frontier in the Pacific* (Oxford: Clarendon Press, 1974).

Stettinius, Edward R., Jr., *Roosevelt and the Russians* (Garden City, NY: Doubleday & Company, Inc., 1949).

Tang, Peter S. H., *Russian and Soviet Policy in Manchuria and Outer Mongolia 1911–1932* (Durham: Duke University Press, 1959).

Thaku, Ramesh and Carlyle Thayer, *Soviet Relations with India and Vietnam* (New York: St. Martin's Press, 1992).

Tilchin, William N., *Theodore Roosevelt and the British Empire: A Study in Presidential Statecraft* (New York: St. Martin's Press, 1997).

Ulam, Adam B., *Expansion & Coexistence: The History of Soviet Foreign Policy 1917–1967* (New York, NY: Frederick A. Praeger, 1968).

United States, Department of State, *Foreign Relations of the United States, 1943, the Conferences of Cairo and Teheran* (Washington, DC: Government Printing Office, 1961).

Wang Shih-han, "May 4th Movement," *China Reconstructs* (Peking, 1962).

Wilbur, C. Martin, ed., Ch'en Kung-po, *The Communist Movement in China* (New York: East Asian Institute, Columbia University, 1960).

Wu Hsiang-hsiang, *E-ti Ch'in-lueh Chung-kuo Shih* (A History of Imperial Russia's Invasion of China) (Taipei: Cheng Chung Book Company, 1954).

ABOUT THE AUTHOR

Bruce A. Elleman received his BA from UC Berkeley in 1982, MA in 1984, MPhil in 1987 and PhD in 1993 at Columbia University. He completed a MSc at the London School of Economics in 1985, and a Master of Arts in National Security and Strategic Studies (with distinction) at the U.S. Naval War College, Newport, Rhode Island, in 2004.

Elleman's dissertation research on Sino-Soviet diplomatic relations was conducted in Russia (1988–89), the People's Republic of China (1990–91), Taiwan (1991–92) and Japan (1992–93). Elleman taught at Texas Christian University, receiving tenure in the History Department. In 2000, Elleman moved to the Center for Naval Warfare Studies at the U.S. Naval War College. In 2013, he was made the William V. Pratt Professor of International History.

Elleman has published 34 books, ranging from Sino-Soviet diplomatic relations, to naval history, to military history. Most recently he has published *Taiwan's Offshore Islands: Pathway or Barrier?* (2019); *The Making of the Modern Chinese Navy: Special Historical Characteristics* (2019); *International Rivalry and Secret Diplomacy in East Asia, 1896-1950* (2019); *A History of the Modern Chinese Navy: 1840-2020* (2021); *Taiwan Straits Standoff: 70 Years of PRC-Taiwan Cross-Strait Tensions* (2022); *Principles of Maritime Power* (2022); and *The United States Navy's Pivot to Asia: The Origins of A Cooperative Strategy for Twenty-First Century Seapower* (2023).

INDEX

Printed in the USA
CPSIA information can be obtained
at www.ICGtesting.com
JSHW022055060923
47842JS00001B/1